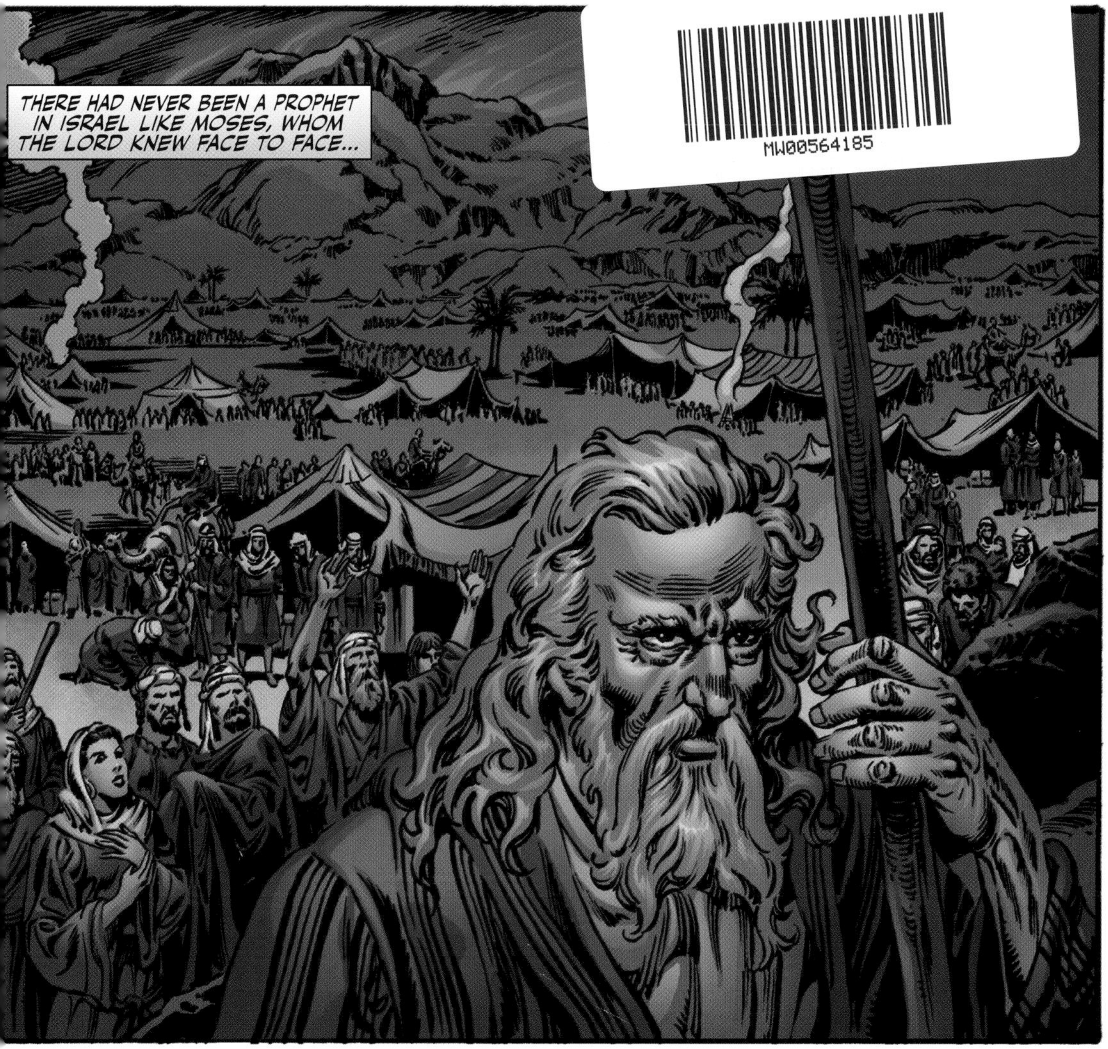
THERE HAD NEVER BEEN A PROPHET IN ISRAEL LIKE MOSES, WHOM THE LORD KNEW FACE TO FACE...

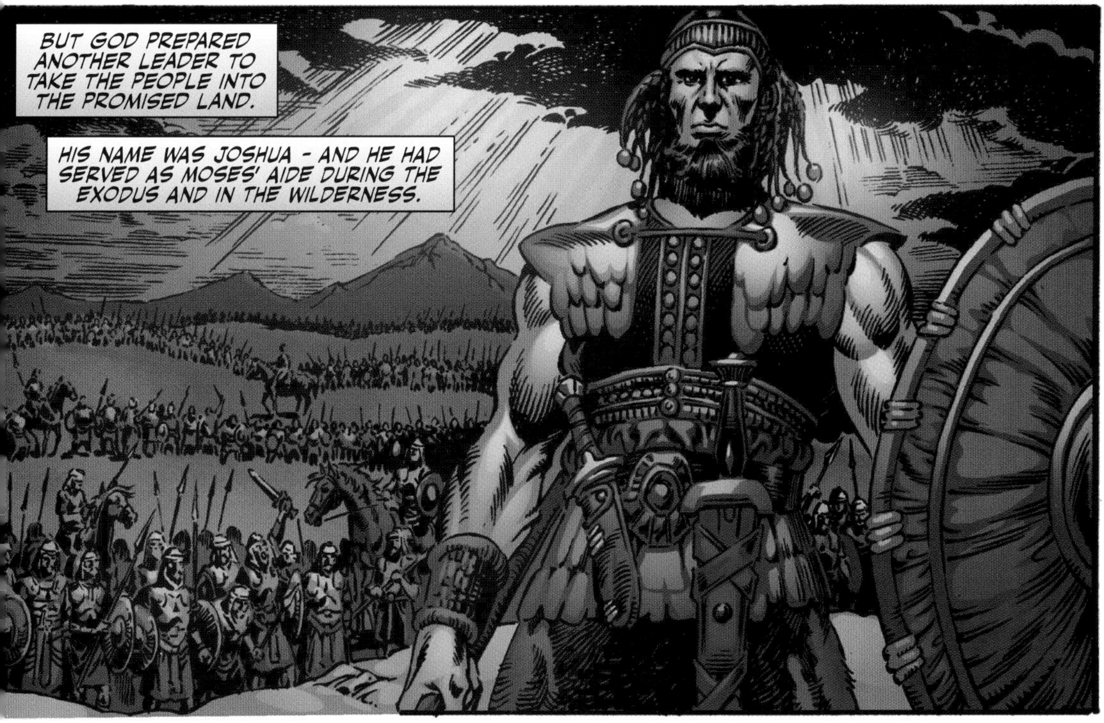
BUT GOD PREPARED ANOTHER LEADER TO TAKE THE PEOPLE INTO THE PROMISED LAND.
HIS NAME WAS JOSHUA - AND HE HAD SERVED AS MOSES' AIDE DURING THE EXODUS AND IN THE WILDERNESS.

DEUTERONOMY 34:8-12

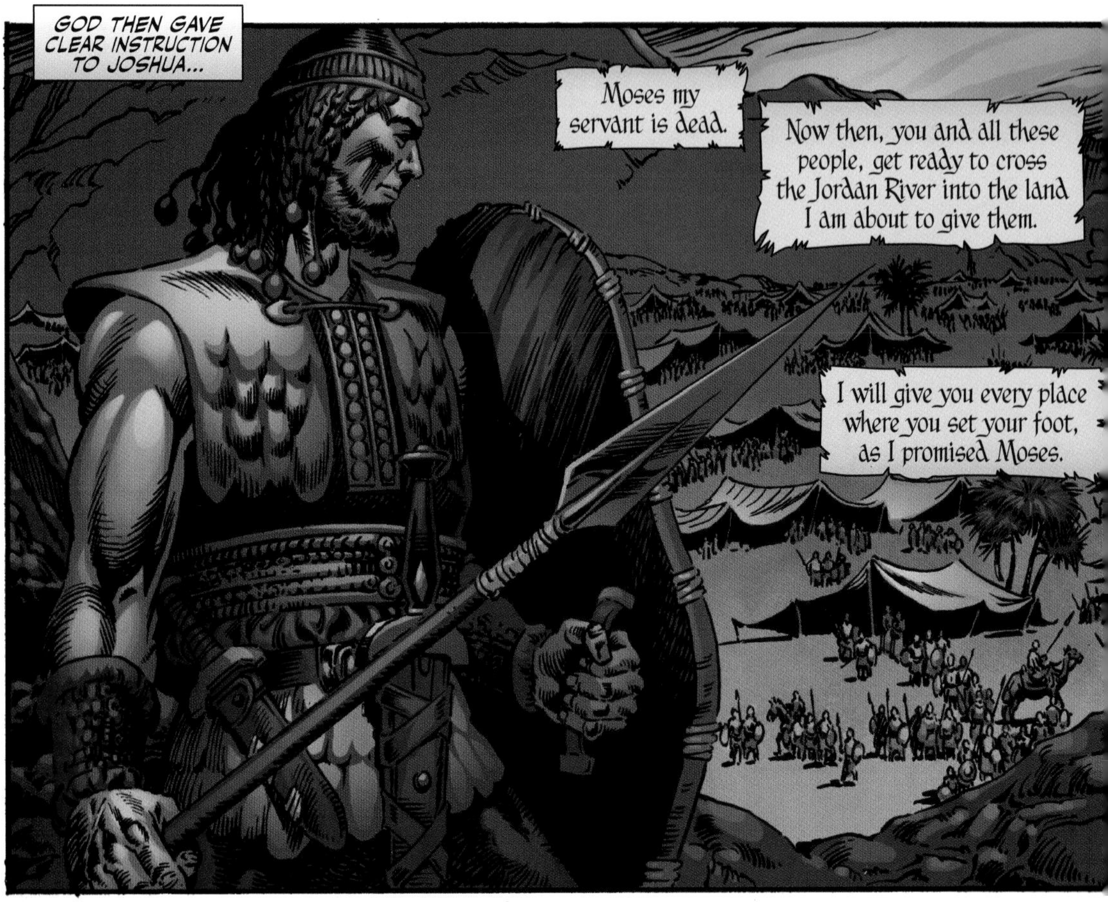
GOD THEN GAVE CLEAR INSTRUCTION TO JOSHUA...
Moses my servant is dead.
Now then, you and all these people, get ready to cross the Jordan River into the land I am about to give them.
I will give you every place where you set your foot, as I promised Moses.

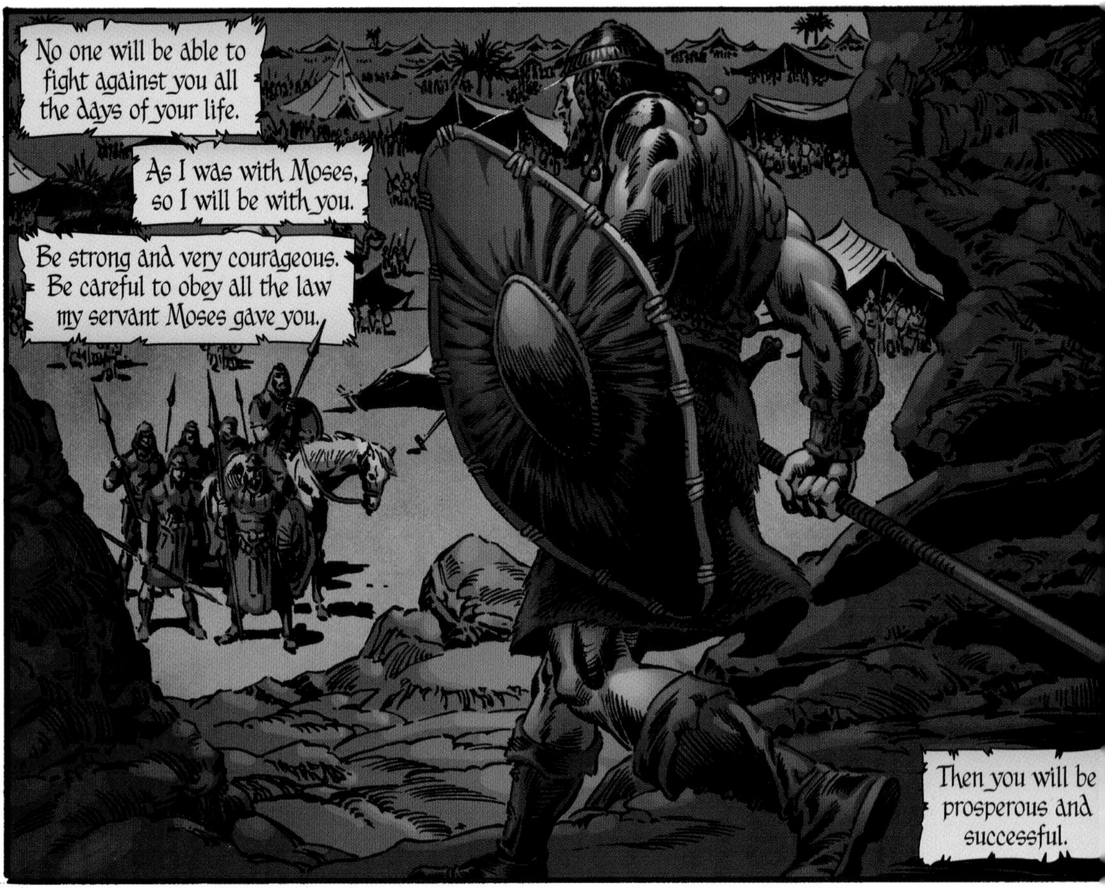
No one will be able to fight against you all the days of your life.
As I was with Moses, so I will be with you.
Be strong and very courageous. Be careful to obey all the law my servant Moses gave you.
Then you will be prosperous and successful.

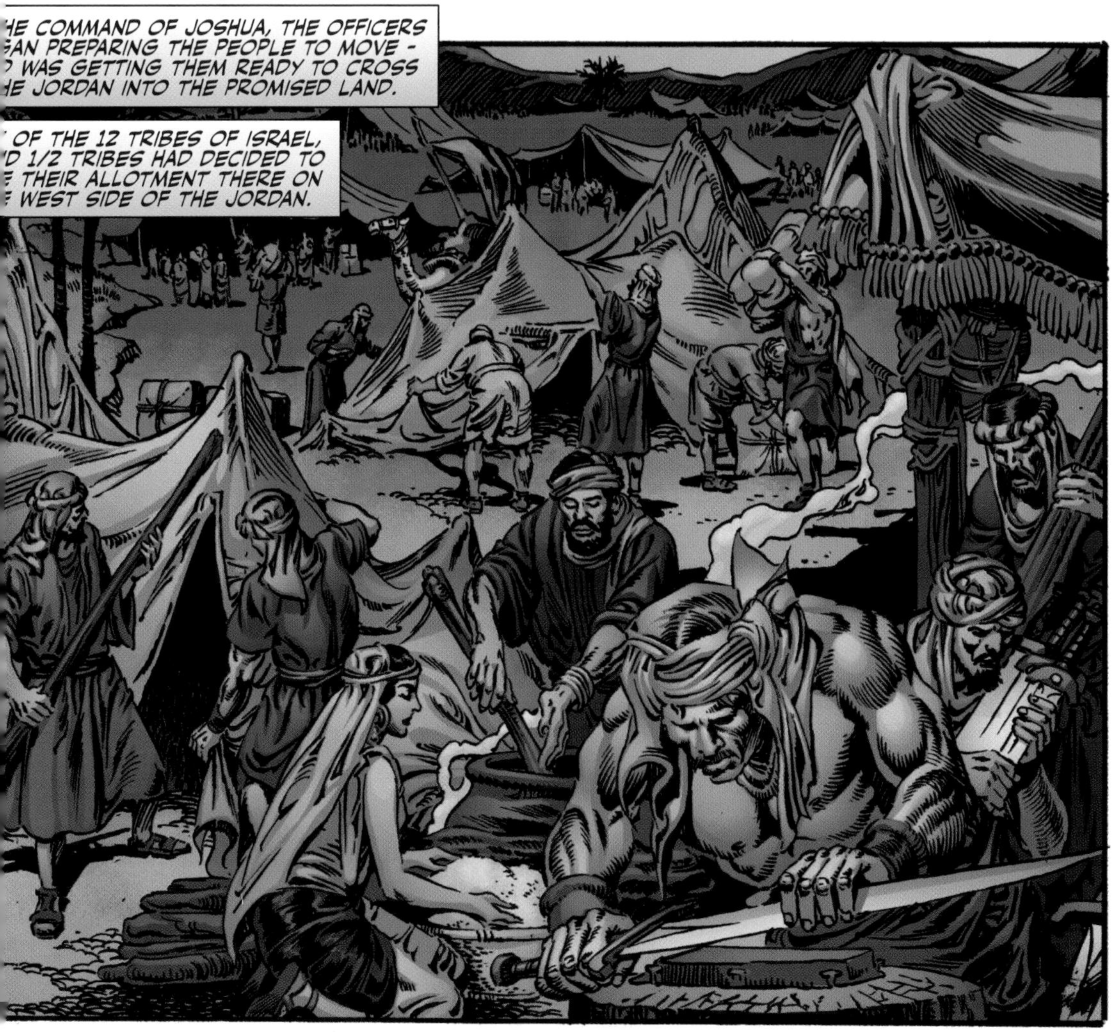
HE COMMAND OF JOSHUA, THE OFFICERS
GAN PREPARING THE PEOPLE TO MOVE -
D WAS GETTING THEM READY TO CROSS
HE JORDAN INTO THE PROMISED LAND.
OF THE 12 TRIBES OF ISRAEL,
D 1/2 TRIBES HAD DECIDED TO
E THEIR ALLOTMENT THERE ON
E WEST SIDE OF THE JORDAN.

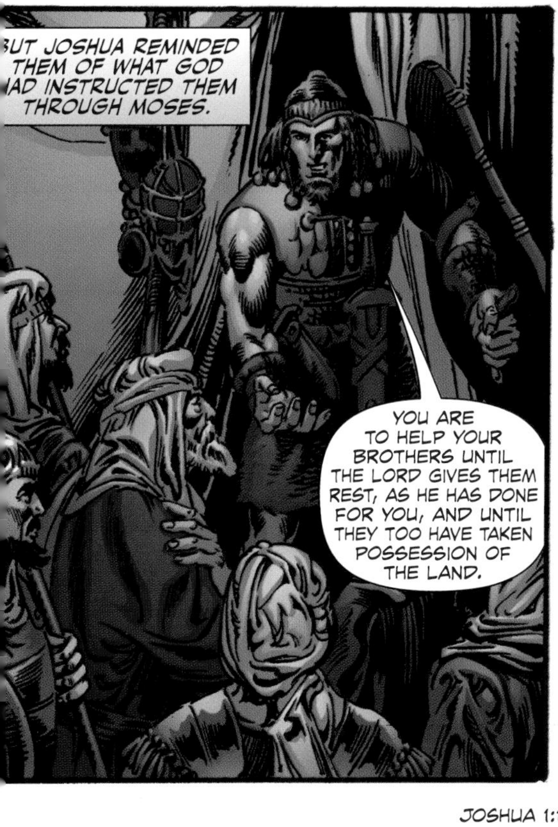
UT JOSHUA REMINDED THEM OF WHAT GOD AD INSTRUCTED THEM THROUGH MOSES.
YOU ARE TO HELP YOUR BROTHERS UNTIL THE LORD GIVES THEM REST, AS HE HAS DONE FOR YOU, AND UNTIL THEY TOO HAVE TAKEN POSSESSION OF THE LAND.

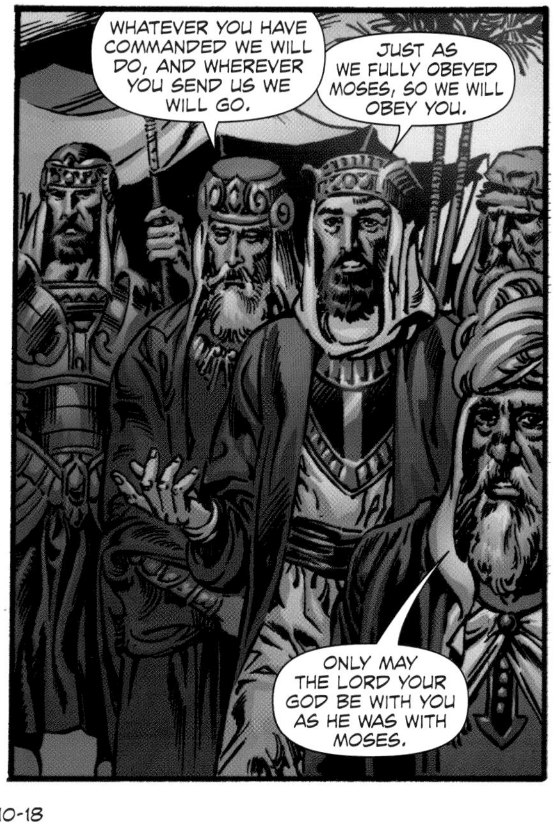
WHATEVER YOU HAVE COMMANDED WE WILL DO, AND WHEREVER YOU SEND US WE WILL GO.
JUST AS WE FULLY OBEYED MOSES, SO WE WILL OBEY YOU.
ONLY MAY THE LORD YOUR GOD BE WITH YOU AS HE WAS WITH MOSES.

JOSHUA 1:10-18

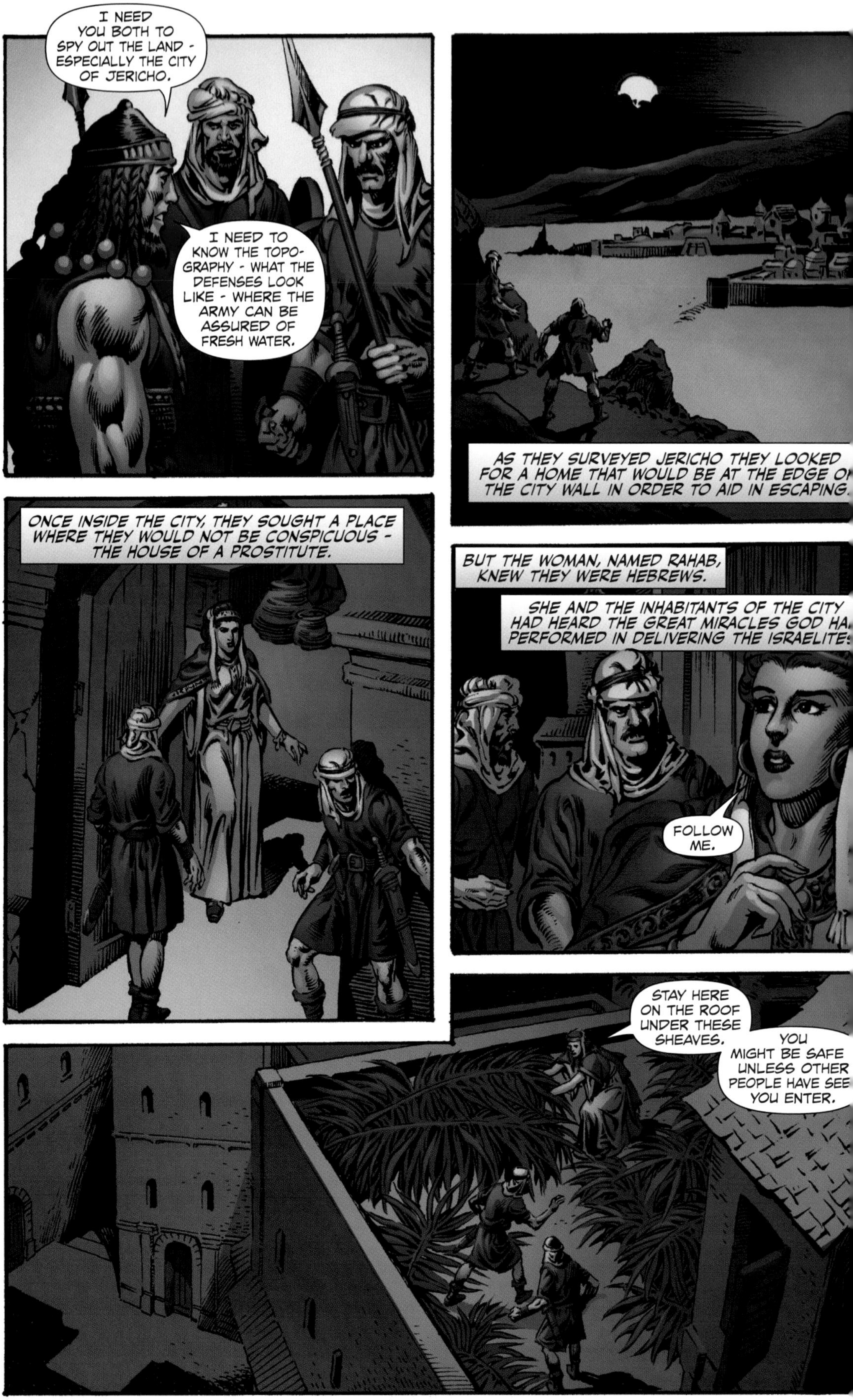

I NEED YOU BOTH TO SPY OUT THE LAND - ESPECIALLY THE CITY OF JERICHO.
I NEED TO KNOW THE TOPOGRAPHY - WHAT THE DEFENSES LOOK LIKE - WHERE THE ARMY CAN BE ASSURED OF FRESH WATER.
AS THEY SURVEYED JERICHO THEY LOOKED FOR A HOME THAT WOULD BE AT THE EDGE OF THE CITY WALL IN ORDER TO AID IN ESCAPING.
ONCE INSIDE THE CITY, THEY SOUGHT A PLACE WHERE THEY WOULD NOT BE CONSPICUOUS - THE HOUSE OF A PROSTITUTE.
BUT THE WOMAN, NAMED RAHAB, KNEW THEY WERE HEBREWS.
SHE AND THE INHABITANTS OF THE CITY HAD HEARD THE GREAT MIRACLES GOD HA PERFORMED IN DELIVERING THE ISRAELITES
FOLLOW ME.
STAY HERE ON THE ROOF UNDER THESE SHEAVES.
YOU MIGHT BE SAFE UNLESS OTHER PEOPLE HAVE SEE YOU ENTER.

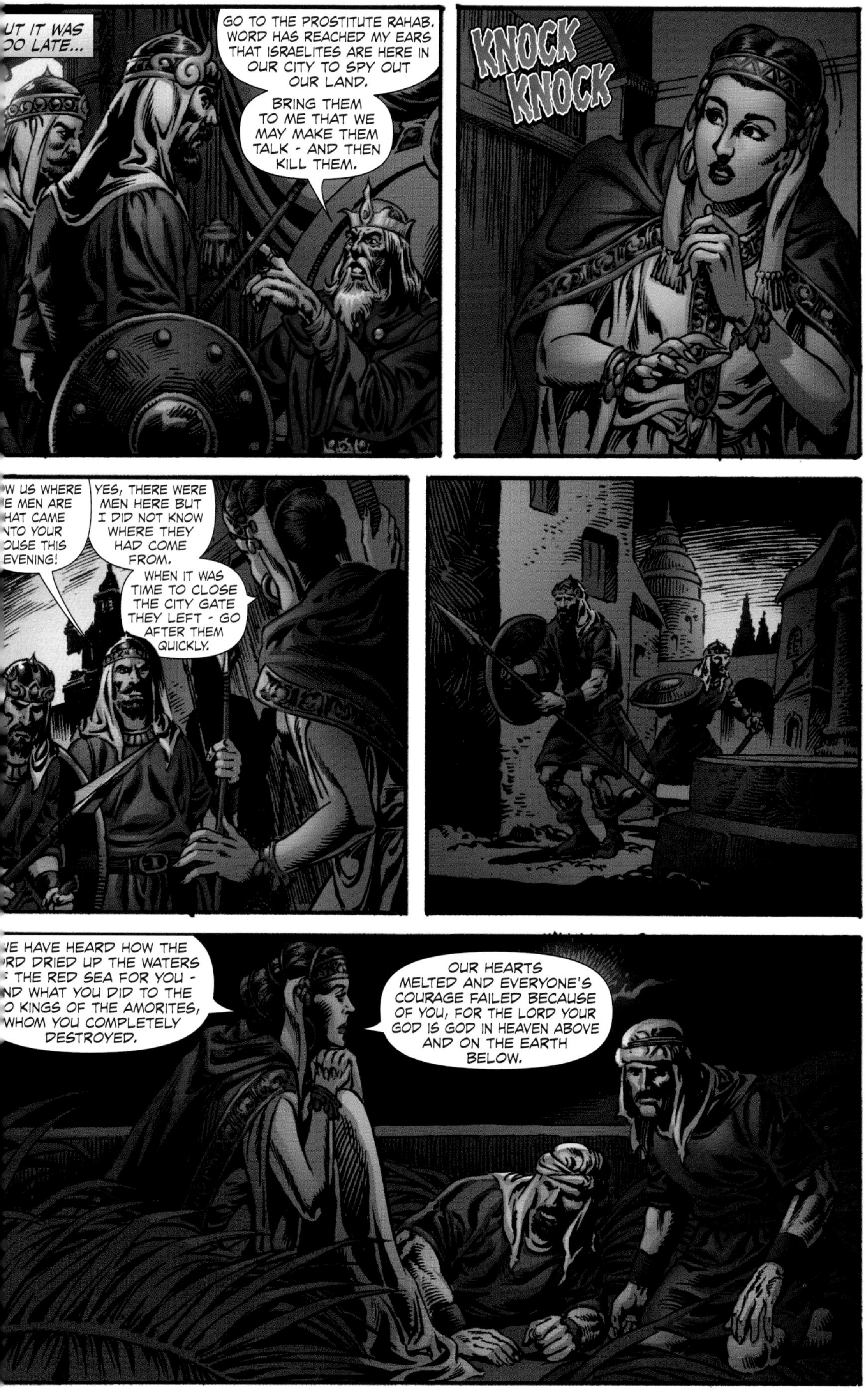
UT IT WAS
OO LATE...
GO TO THE PROSTITUTE RAHAB. WORD HAS REACHED MY EARS THAT ISRAELITES ARE HERE IN OUR CITY TO SPY OUT OUR LAND.
BRING THEM TO ME THAT WE MAY MAKE THEM TALK - AND THEN KILL THEM.
KNOCK KNOCK
W US WHERE E MEN ARE HAT CAME NTO YOUR OUSE THIS EVENING!
YES, THERE WERE MEN HERE BUT I DID NOT KNOW WHERE THEY HAD COME FROM.
WHEN IT WAS TIME TO CLOSE THE CITY GATE THEY LEFT - GO AFTER THEM QUICKLY.
E HAVE HEARD HOW THE RD DRIED UP THE WATERS THE RED SEA FOR YOU - ND WHAT YOU DID TO THE O KINGS OF THE AMORITES, WHOM YOU COMPLETELY DESTROYED.
OUR HEARTS MELTED AND EVERYONE'S COURAGE FAILED BECAUSE OF YOU, FOR THE LORD YOUR GOD IS GOD IN HEAVEN ABOVE AND ON THE EARTH BELOW.

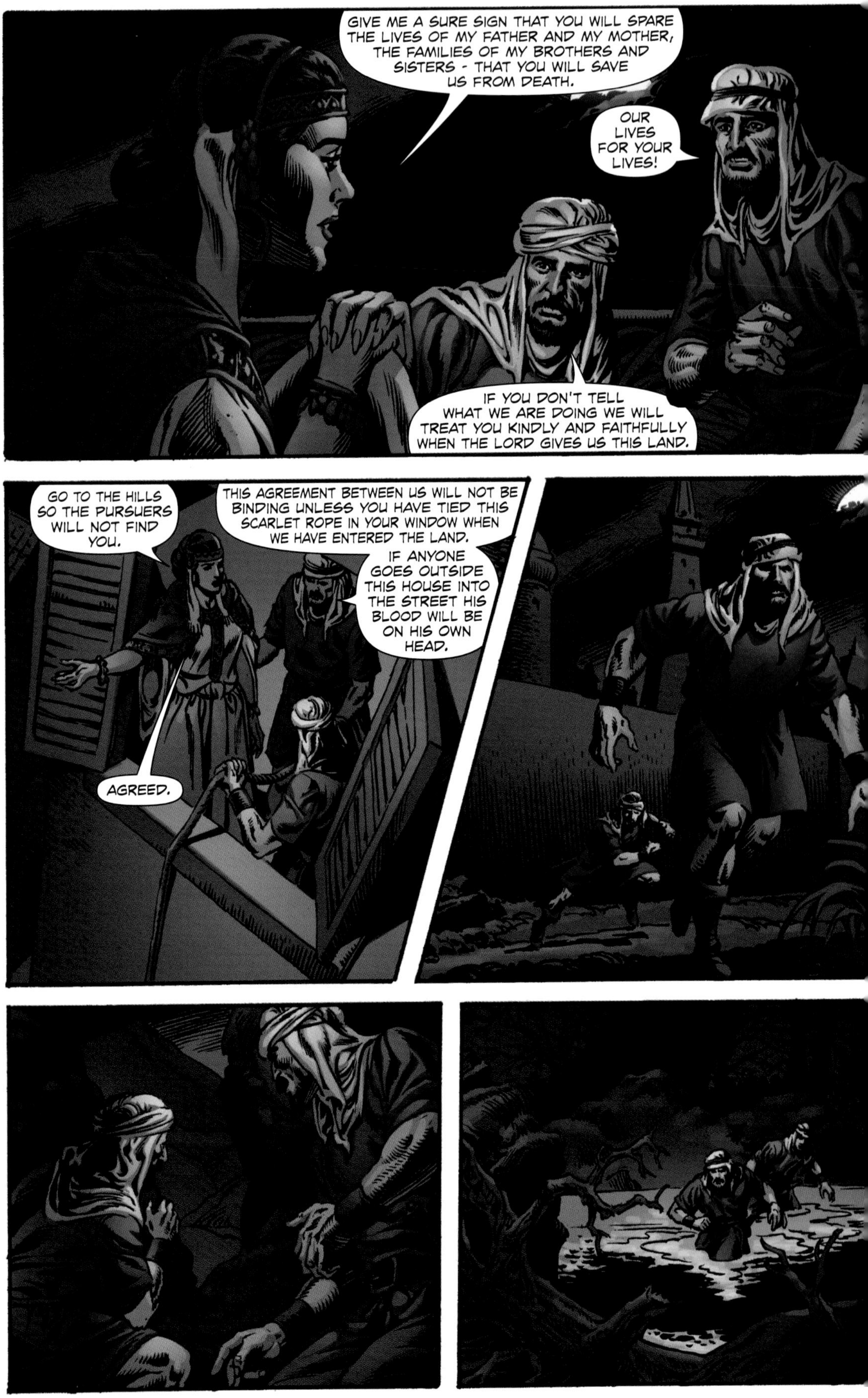
GIVE ME A SURE SIGN THAT YOU WILL SPARE THE LIVES OF MY FATHER AND MY MOTHER, THE FAMILIES OF MY BROTHERS AND SISTERS - THAT YOU WILL SAVE US FROM DEATH.
OUR LIVES FOR YOUR LIVES!
IF YOU DON'T TELL WHAT WE ARE DOING WE WILL TREAT YOU KINDLY AND FAITHFULLY WHEN THE LORD GIVES US THIS LAND.
GO TO THE HILLS SO THE PURSUERS WILL NOT FIND YOU.
THIS AGREEMENT BETWEEN US WILL NOT BE BINDING UNLESS YOU HAVE TIED THIS SCARLET ROPE IN YOUR WINDOW WHEN WE HAVE ENTERED THE LAND.
IF ANYONE GOES OUTSIDE THIS HOUSE INTO THE STREET HIS BLOOD WILL BE ON HIS OWN HEAD.
AGREED.

JOSHUA 2:12-23

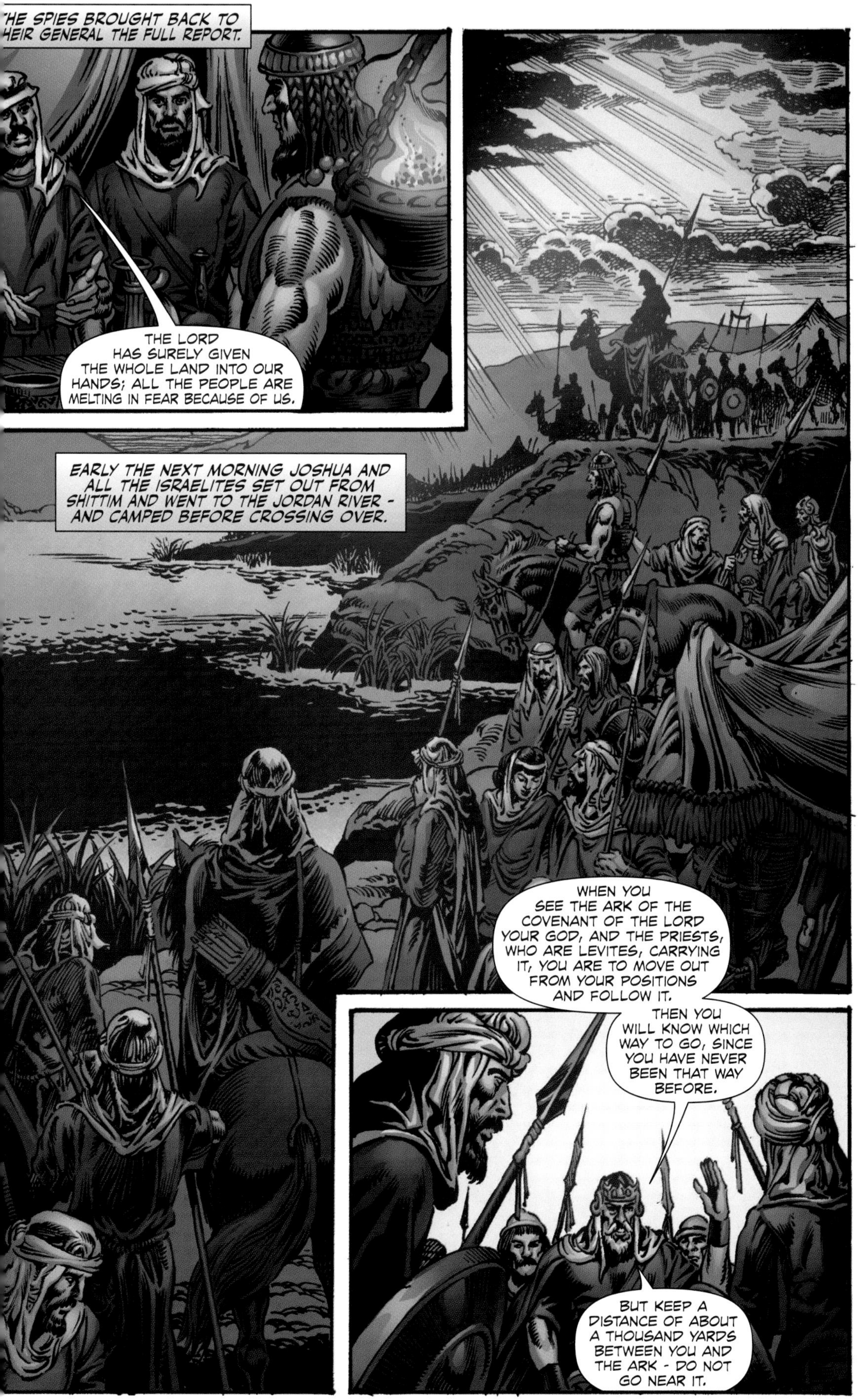

THE SPIES BROUGHT BACK TO THEIR GENERAL THE FULL REPORT.
THE LORD HAS SURELY GIVEN THE WHOLE LAND INTO OUR HANDS; ALL THE PEOPLE ARE MELTING IN FEAR BECAUSE OF US.
EARLY THE NEXT MORNING JOSHUA AND ALL THE ISRAELITES SET OUT FROM SHITTIM AND WENT TO THE JORDAN RIVER - AND CAMPED BEFORE CROSSING OVER.
WHEN YOU SEE THE ARK OF THE COVENANT OF THE LORD YOUR GOD, AND THE PRIESTS, WHO ARE LEVITES, CARRYING IT, YOU ARE TO MOVE OUT FROM YOUR POSITIONS AND FOLLOW IT.
THEN YOU WILL KNOW WHICH WAY TO GO, SINCE YOU HAVE NEVER BEEN THAT WAY BEFORE.
BUT KEEP A DISTANCE OF ABOUT A THOUSAND YARDS BETWEEN YOU AND THE ARK - DO NOT GO NEAR IT.

JOSHUA 2:23 - 3:4

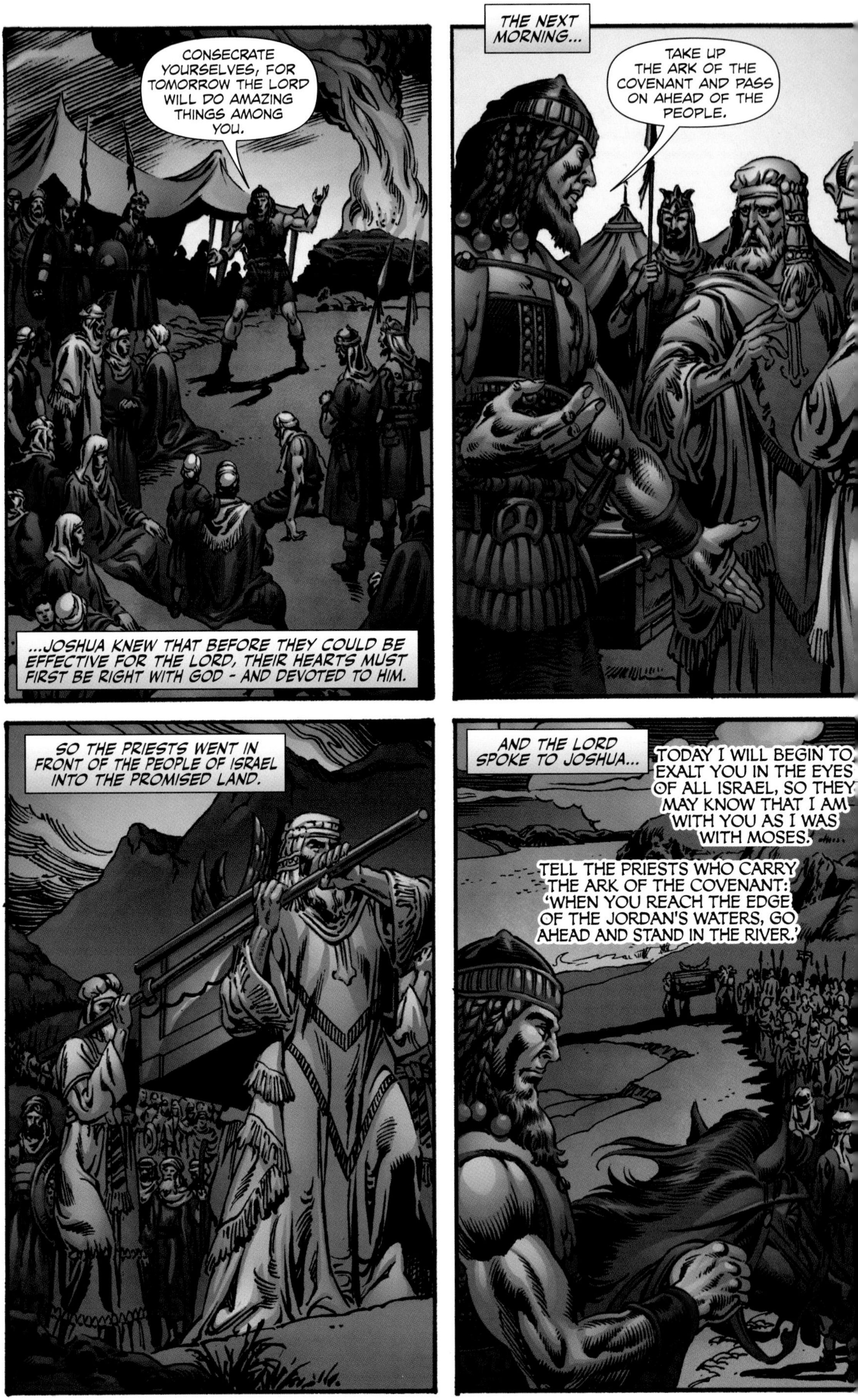
CONSECRATE YOURSELVES, FOR TOMORROW THE LORD WILL DO AMAZING THINGS AMONG YOU.
...JOSHUA KNEW THAT BEFORE THEY COULD BE EFFECTIVE FOR THE LORD, THEIR HEARTS MUST FIRST BE RIGHT WITH GOD - AND DEVOTED TO HIM.
THE NEXT MORNING...
TAKE UP THE ARK OF THE COVENANT AND PASS ON AHEAD OF THE PEOPLE.
SO THE PRIESTS WENT IN FRONT OF THE PEOPLE OF ISRAEL INTO THE PROMISED LAND.
AND THE LORD SPOKE TO JOSHUA...
TODAY I WILL BEGIN TO EXALT YOU IN THE EYES OF ALL ISRAEL, SO THEY MAY KNOW THAT I AM WITH YOU AS I WAS WITH MOSES.
TELL THE PRIESTS WHO CARRY THE ARK OF THE COVENANT: 'WHEN YOU REACH THE EDGE OF THE JORDAN'S WATERS, GO AHEAD AND STAND IN THE RIVER.'

JOSHUA: 3:5-7

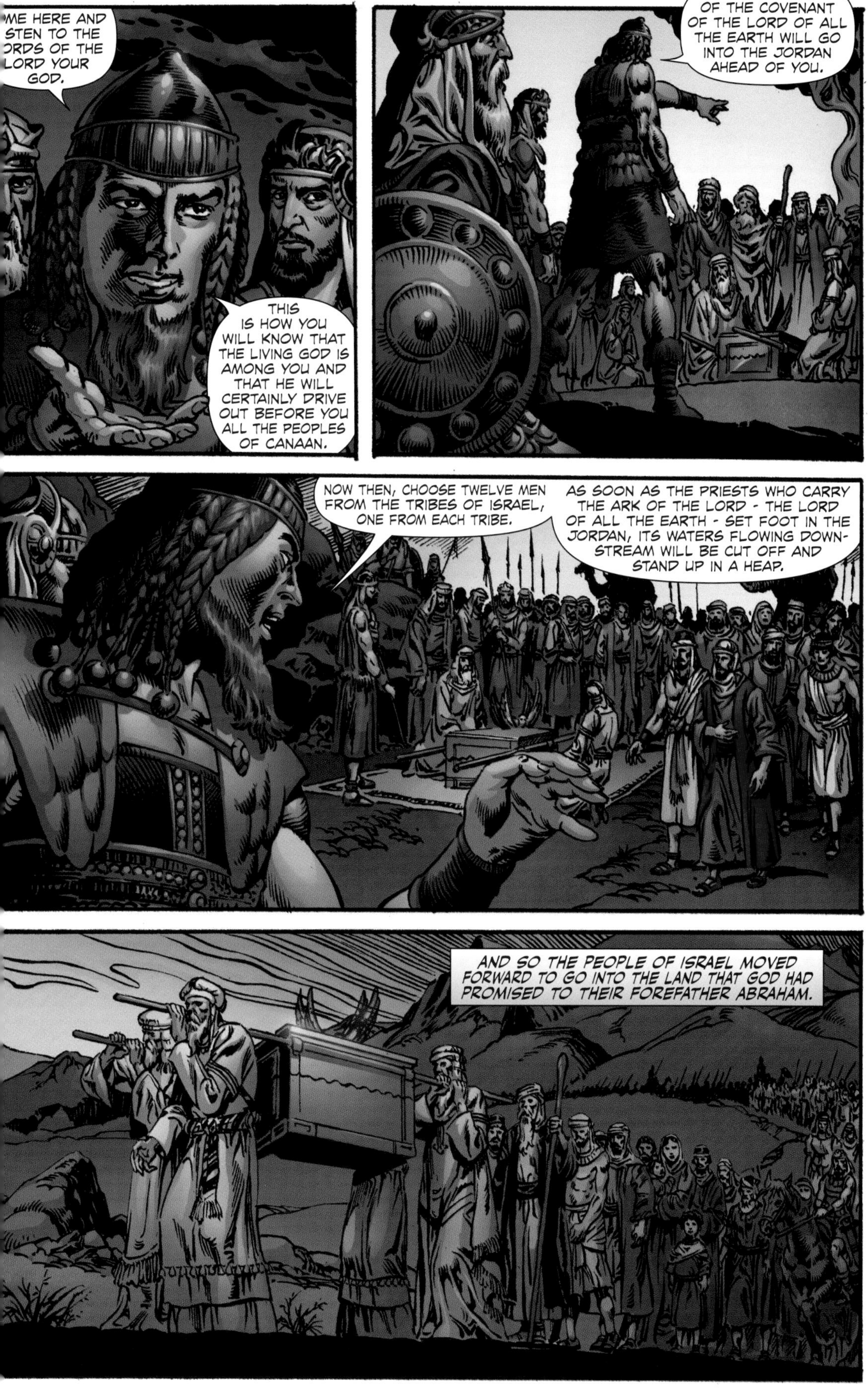
ME HERE AND
STEN TO THE
ORDS OF THE
LORD YOUR
GOD.
THIS IS HOW YOU WILL KNOW THAT THE LIVING GOD IS AMONG YOU AND THAT HE WILL CERTAINLY DRIVE OUT BEFORE YOU ALL THE PEOPLES OF CANAAN.
SEE, THE ARK OF THE COVENANT OF THE LORD OF ALL THE EARTH WILL GO INTO THE JORDAN AHEAD OF YOU.
NOW THEN, CHOOSE TWELVE MEN FROM THE TRIBES OF ISRAEL, ONE FROM EACH TRIBE.
AS SOON AS THE PRIESTS WHO CARRY THE ARK OF THE LORD - THE LORD OF ALL THE EARTH - SET FOOT IN THE JORDAN, ITS WATERS FLOWING DOWN-STREAM WILL BE CUT OFF AND STAND UP IN A HEAP.
AND SO THE PEOPLE OF ISRAEL MOVED FORWARD TO GO INTO THE LAND THAT GOD HAD PROMISED TO THEIR FOREFATHER ABRAHAM.

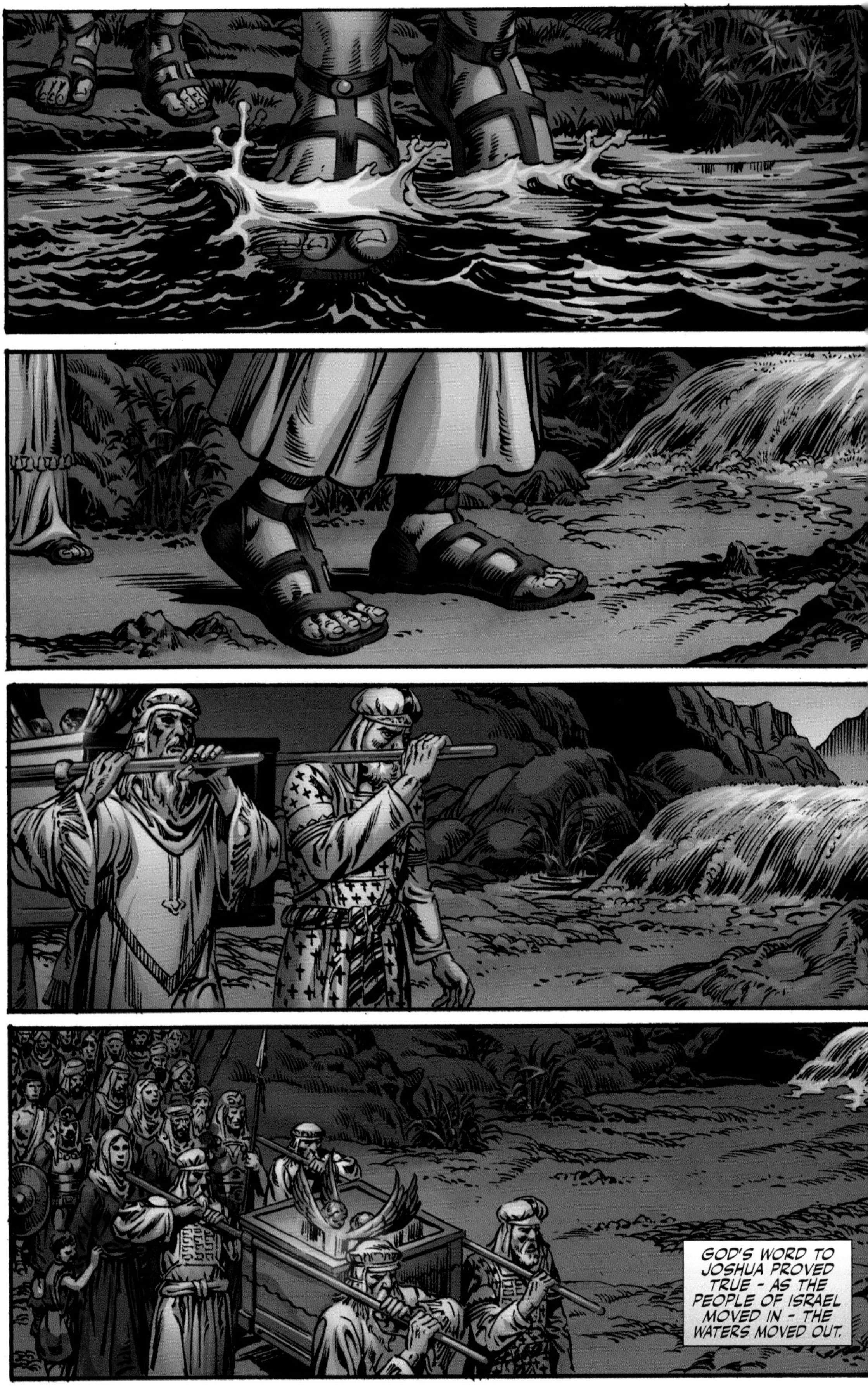
GOD'S WORD TO JOSHUA PROVED TRUE - AS THE PEOPLE OF ISRAEL MOVED IN - THE WATERS MOVED OUT.

JOSHUA 3:15

THE ENTIRE NATION OF ISRAEL WAS ABLE TO PASS THROUGH AS THE PRIESTS STOOD IN THE DRY RIVER BED.

THE LORD THEN DIRECTED JOSHUA TO HAVE TWELVE MEN GET STONES FROM THE MIDDLE OF THE JORDAN RIVER TO SERVE AS A SIGN.

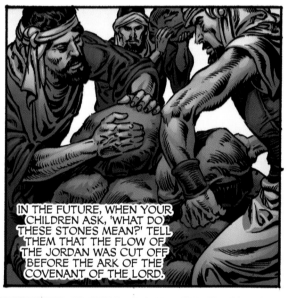

IN THE FUTURE, WHEN YOUR CHILDREN ASK, 'WHAT DO THESE STONES MEAN?' TELL THEM THAT THE FLOW OF THE JORDAN WAS CUT OFF BEFORE THE ARK OF THE COVENANT OF THE LORD.

THESE STONES ARE TO BE A MEMORIAL TO THE PEOPLE OF ISRAEL FOREVER.

THAT DAY THE LORD EXALTED JOSHUA IN THE SIGHT OF ALL ISRAEL; AND THEY REVERED HIM - JUST AS THEY HAD REVERED MOSES.

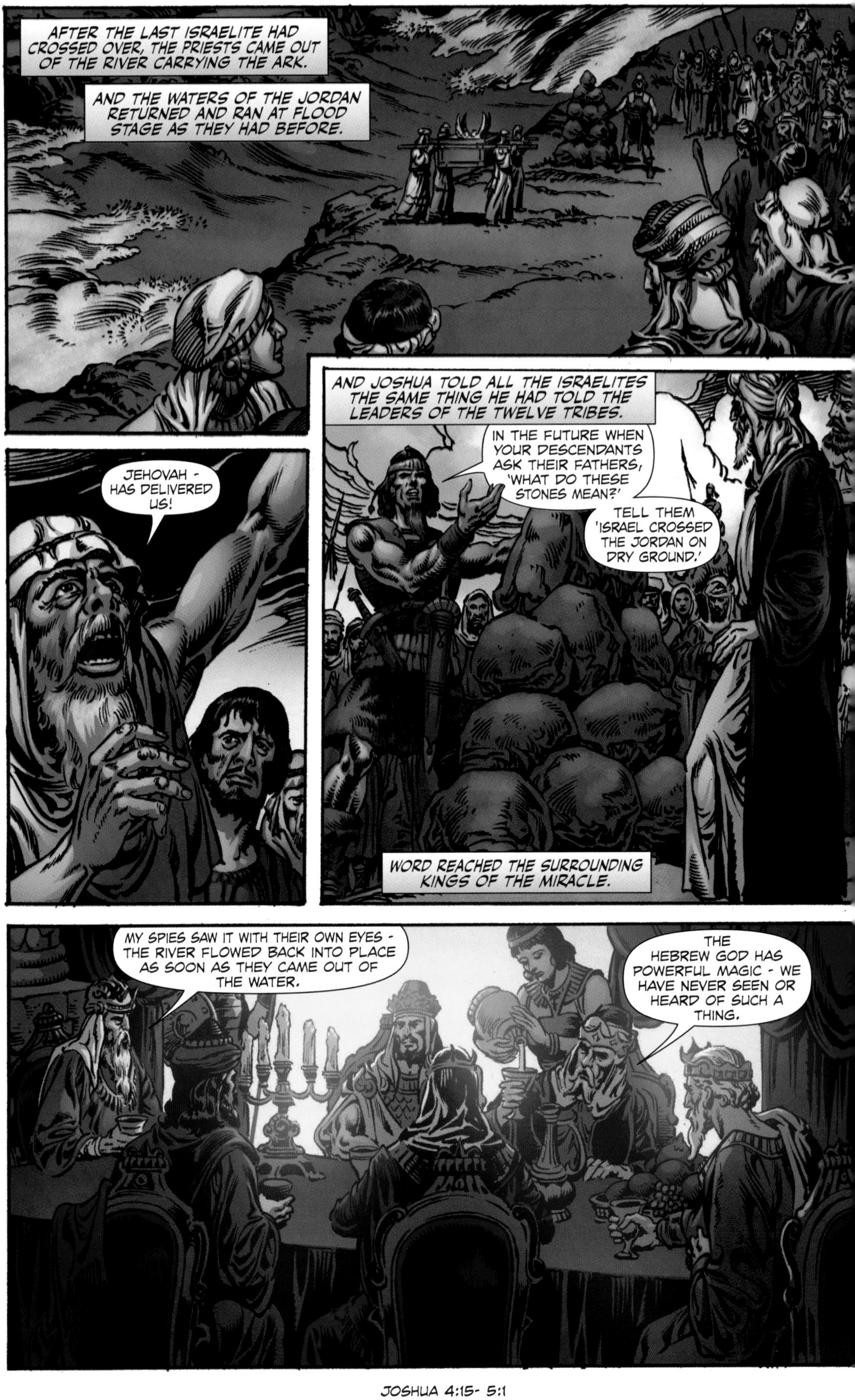
AFTER THE LAST ISRAELITE HAD CROSSED OVER, THE PRIESTS CAME OUT OF THE RIVER CARRYING THE ARK.
AND THE WATERS OF THE JORDAN RETURNED AND RAN AT FLOOD STAGE AS THEY HAD BEFORE.
JEHOVAH - HAS DELIVERED US!
AND JOSHUA TOLD ALL THE ISRAELITES THE SAME THING HE HAD TOLD THE LEADERS OF THE TWELVE TRIBES.
IN THE FUTURE WHEN YOUR DESCENDANTS ASK THEIR FATHERS, 'WHAT DO THESE STONES MEAN?'
TELL THEM 'ISRAEL CROSSED THE JORDAN ON DRY GROUND.'
WORD REACHED THE SURROUNDING KINGS OF THE MIRACLE.
MY SPIES SAW IT WITH THEIR OWN EYES - THE RIVER FLOWED BACK INTO PLACE AS SOON AS THEY CAME OUT OF THE WATER.
THE HEBREW GOD HAS POWERFUL MAGIC - WE HAVE NEVER SEEN OR HEARD OF SUCH A THING.

JOSHUA 4:15- 5:1

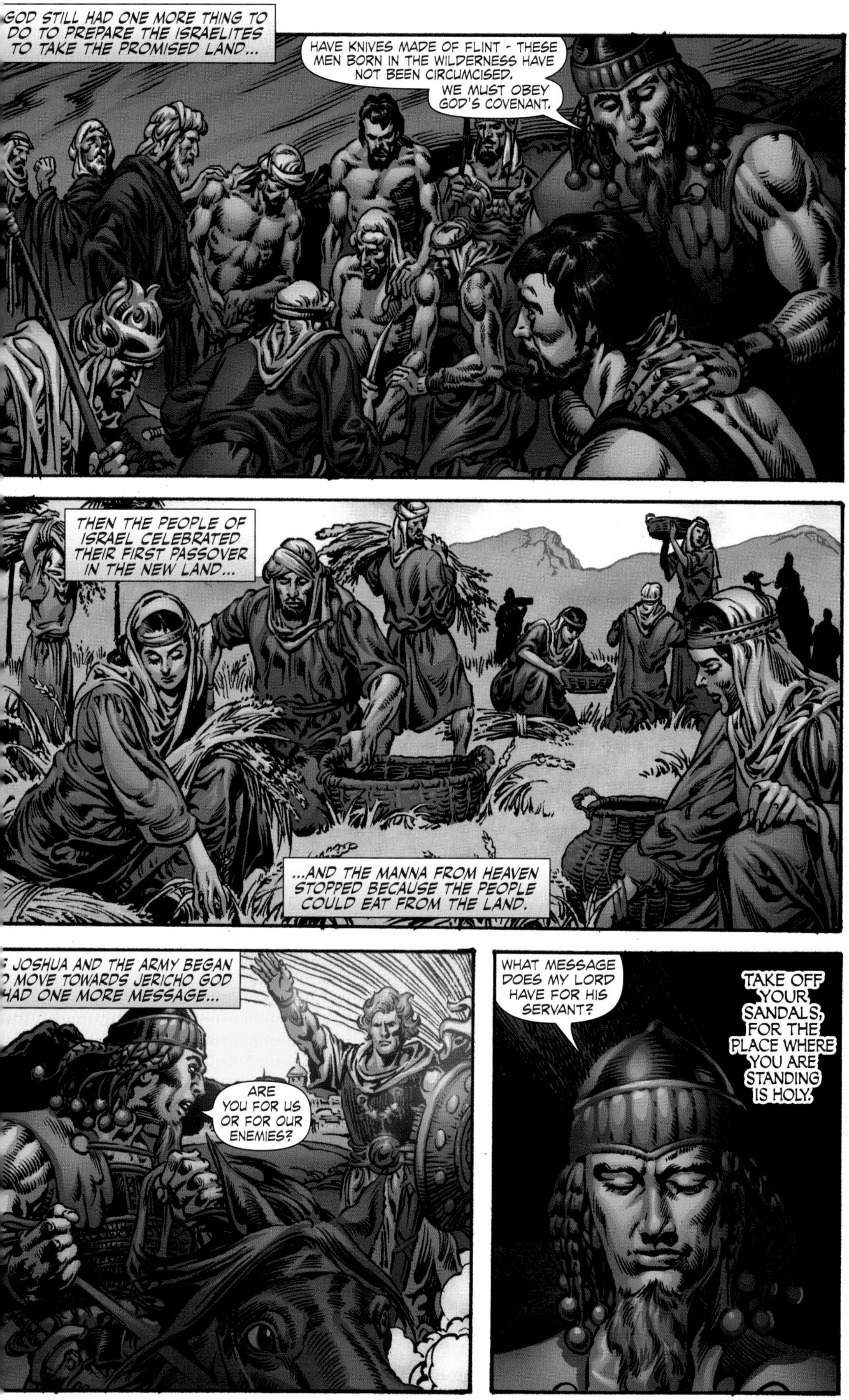
GOD STILL HAD ONE MORE THING TO DO TO PREPARE THE ISRAELITES TO TAKE THE PROMISED LAND...
HAVE KNIVES MADE OF FLINT - THESE MEN BORN IN THE WILDERNESS HAVE NOT BEEN CIRCUMCISED.
WE MUST OBEY GOD'S COVENANT.
THEN THE PEOPLE OF ISRAEL CELEBRATED THEIR FIRST PASSOVER IN THE NEW LAND...
...AND THE MANNA FROM HEAVEN STOPPED BECAUSE THE PEOPLE COULD EAT FROM THE LAND.
JOSHUA AND THE ARMY BEGAN
MOVE TOWARDS JERICHO GOD
HAD ONE MORE MESSAGE...
ARE YOU FOR US OR FOR OUR ENEMIES?
WHAT MESSAGE DOES MY LORD HAVE FOR HIS SERVANT?
TAKE OFF YOUR SANDALS, FOR THE PLACE WHERE YOU ARE STANDING IS HOLY.

JOSHUA 5:2-15

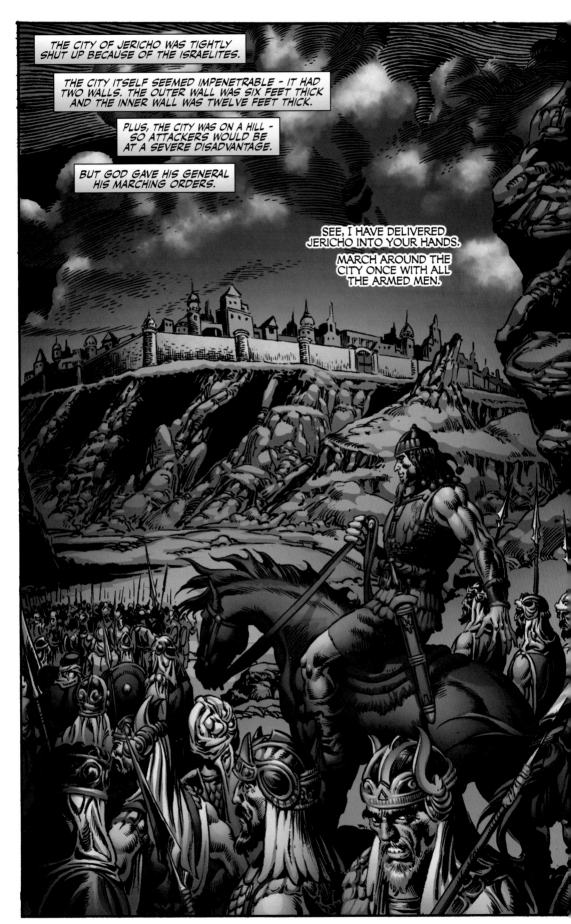

THE CITY OF JERICHO WAS TIGHTLY SHUT UP BECAUSE OF THE ISRAELITES.

THE CITY ITSELF SEEMED IMPENETRABLE – IT HAD TWO WALLS. THE OUTER WALL WAS SIX FEET THICK AND THE INNER WALL WAS TWELVE FEET THICK.

PLUS, THE CITY WAS ON A HILL – SO ATTACKERS WOULD BE AT A SEVERE DISADVANTAGE.

BUT GOD GAVE HIS GENERAL HIS MARCHING ORDERS.

SEE, I HAVE DELIVERED JERICHO INTO YOUR HANDS.

MARCH AROUND THE CITY ONCE WITH ALL THE ARMED MEN.

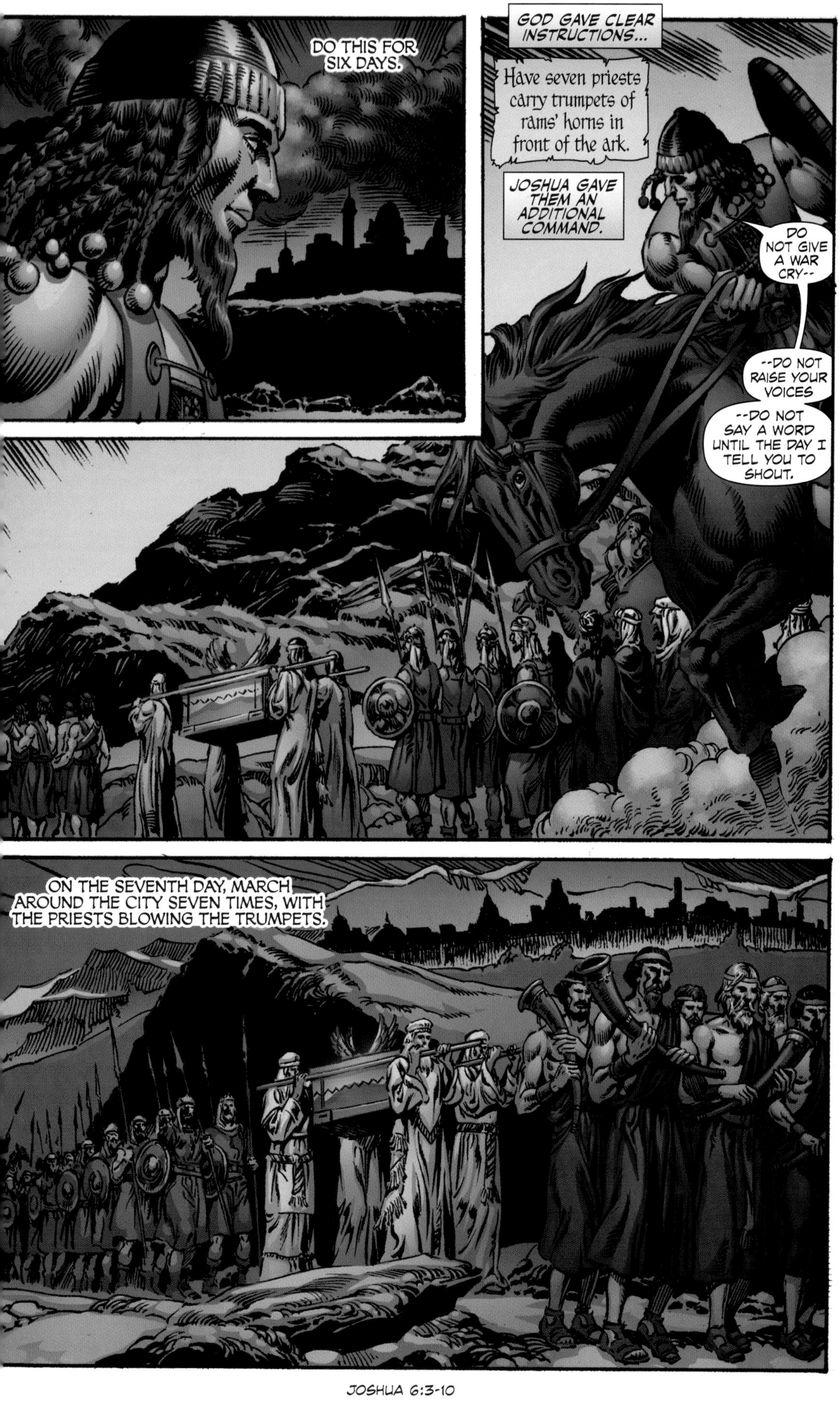
DO THIS FOR SIX DAYS.
GOD GAVE CLEAR INSTRUCTIONS...
Have seven priests carry trumpets of rams' horns in front of the ark.
JOSHUA GAVE THEM AN ADDITIONAL COMMAND.
DO NOT GIVE A WAR CRY--
--DO NOT RAISE YOUR VOICES
--DO NOT SAY A WORD UNTIL THE DAY I TELL YOU TO SHOUT.
ON THE SEVENTH DAY, MARCH AROUND THE CITY SEVEN TIMES, WITH THE PRIESTS BLOWING THE TRUMPETS.

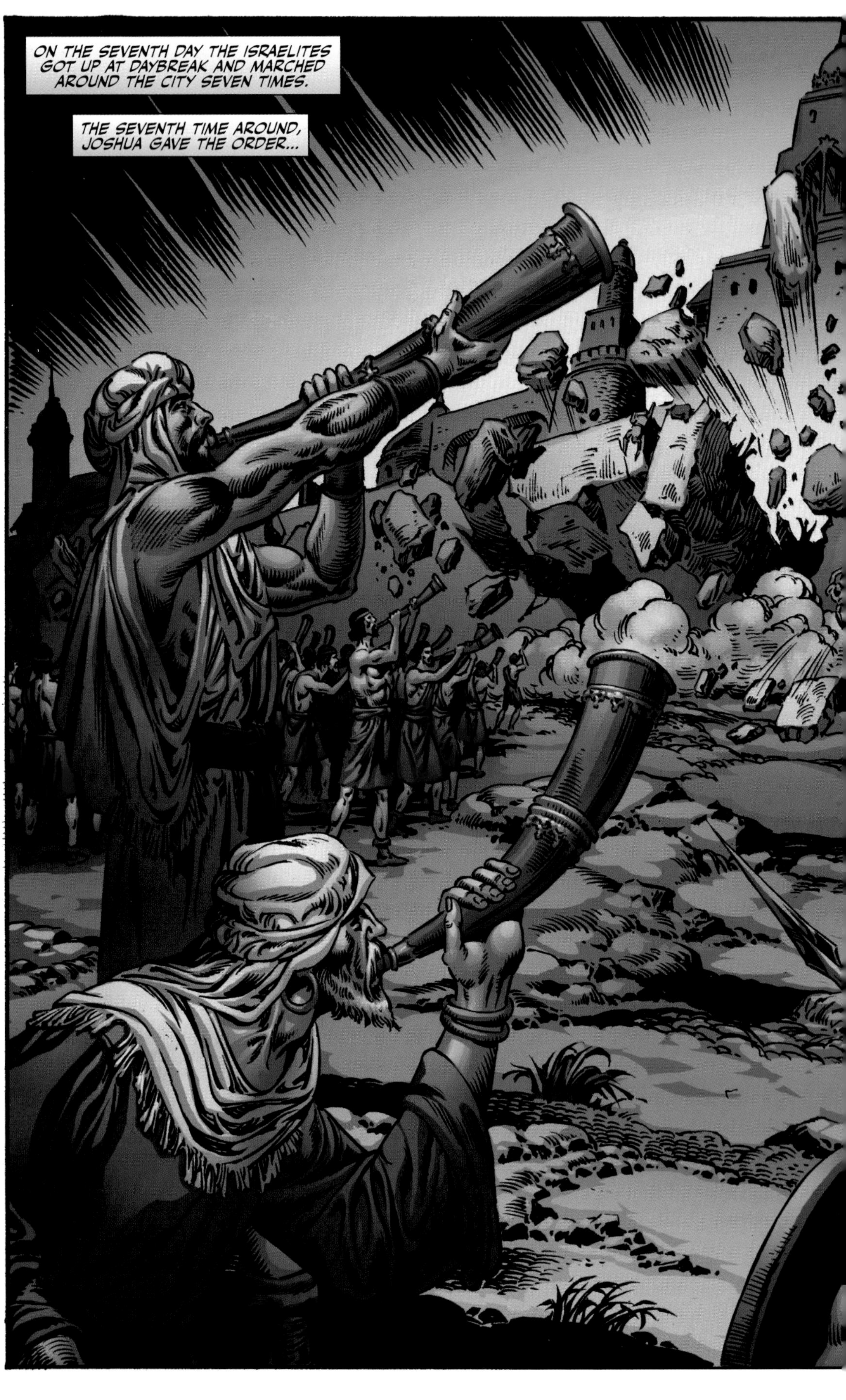
ON THE SEVENTH DAY THE ISRAELITES GOT UP AT DAYBREAK AND MARCHED AROUND THE CITY SEVEN TIMES.
THE SEVENTH TIME AROUND, JOSHUA GAVE THE ORDER...

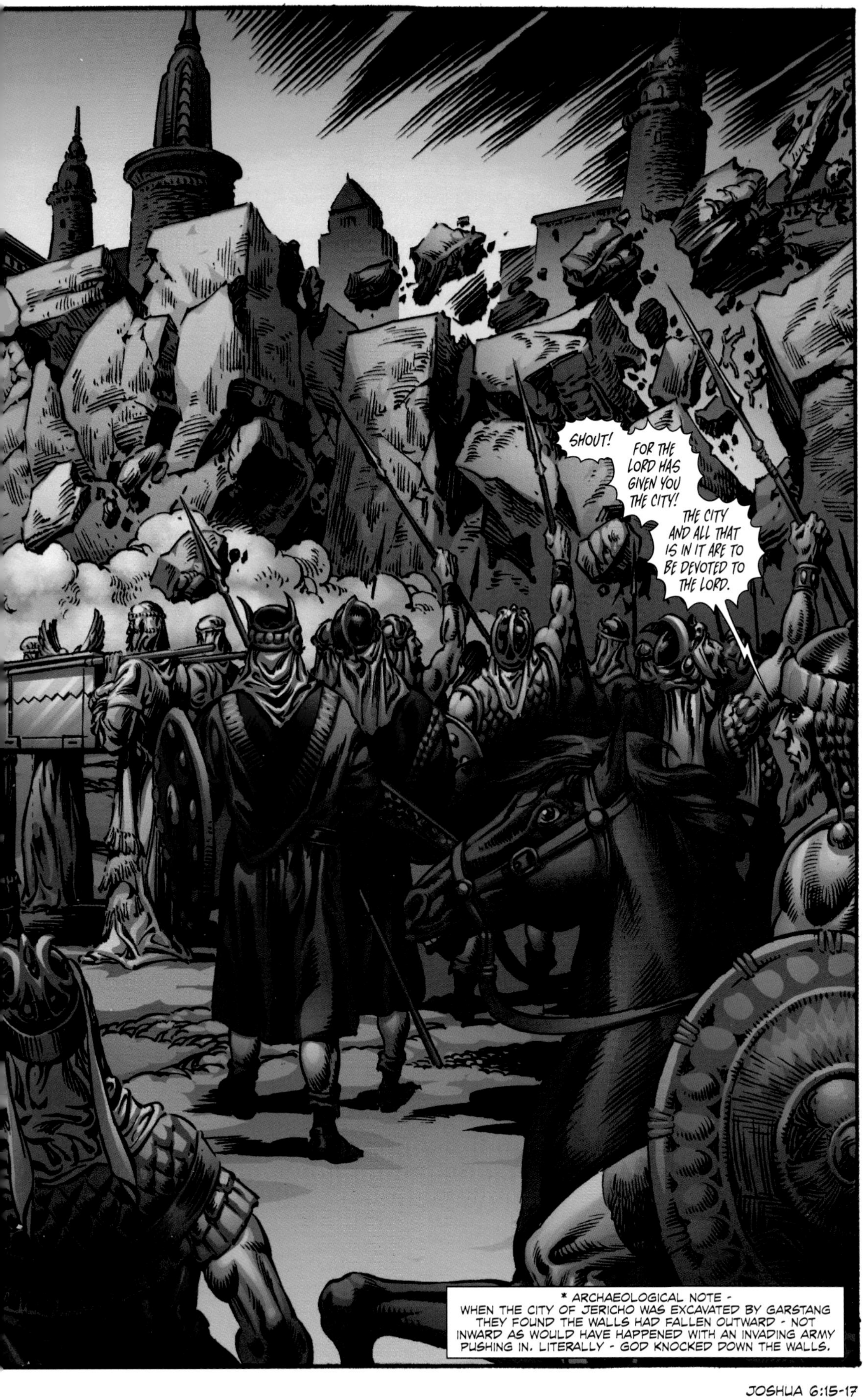
SHOUT!
FOR THE LORD HAS GIVEN YOU THE CITY!
THE CITY AND ALL THAT IS IN IT ARE TO BE DEVOTED TO THE LORD.
* ARCHAEOLOGICAL NOTE - WHEN THE CITY OF JERICHO WAS EXCAVATED BY GARSTANG THEY FOUND THE WALLS HAD FALLEN OUTWARD - NOT INWARD AS WOULD HAVE HAPPENED WITH AN INVADING ARMY PUSHING IN. LITERALLY - GOD KNOCKED DOWN THE WALLS.

JOSHUA 6:15-17

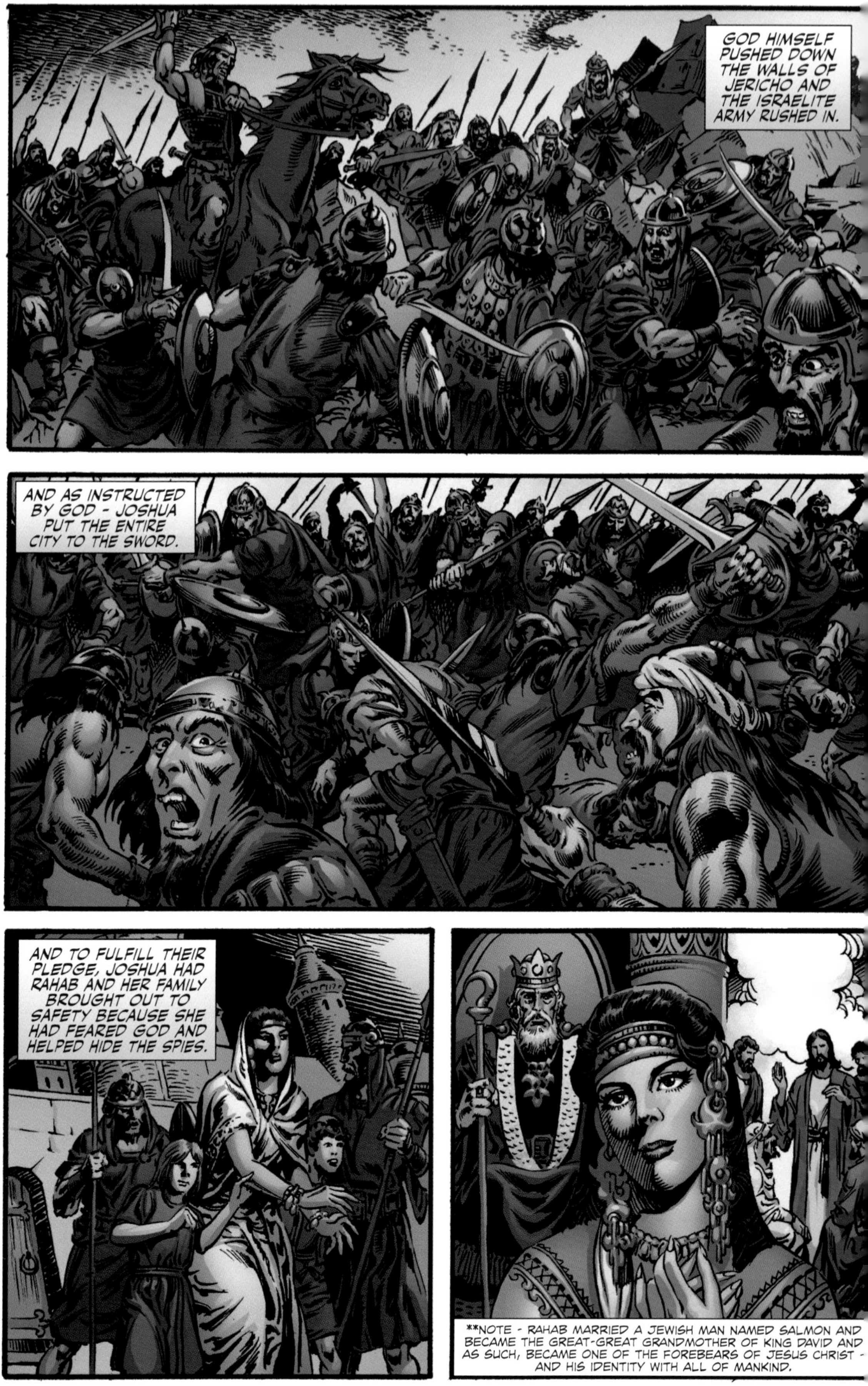
GOD HIMSELF PUSHED DOWN THE WALLS OF JERICHO AND THE ISRAELITE ARMY RUSHED IN.
AND AS INSTRUCTED BY GOD - JOSHUA PUT THE ENTIRE CITY TO THE SWORD.
AND TO FULFILL THEIR PLEDGE, JOSHUA HAD RAHAB AND HER FAMILY BROUGHT OUT TO SAFETY BECAUSE SHE HAD FEARED GOD AND HELPED HIDE THE SPIES.
**NOTE - RAHAB MARRIED A JEWISH MAN NAMED SALMON AND BECAME THE GREAT-GREAT GRANDMOTHER OF KING DAVID AND AS SUCH, BECAME ONE OF THE FOREBEARS OF JESUS CHRIST - AND HIS IDENTITY WITH ALL OF MANKIND.

JOSHUA 6:17-25, HEBREWS 11:31, JAMES 2:24-26

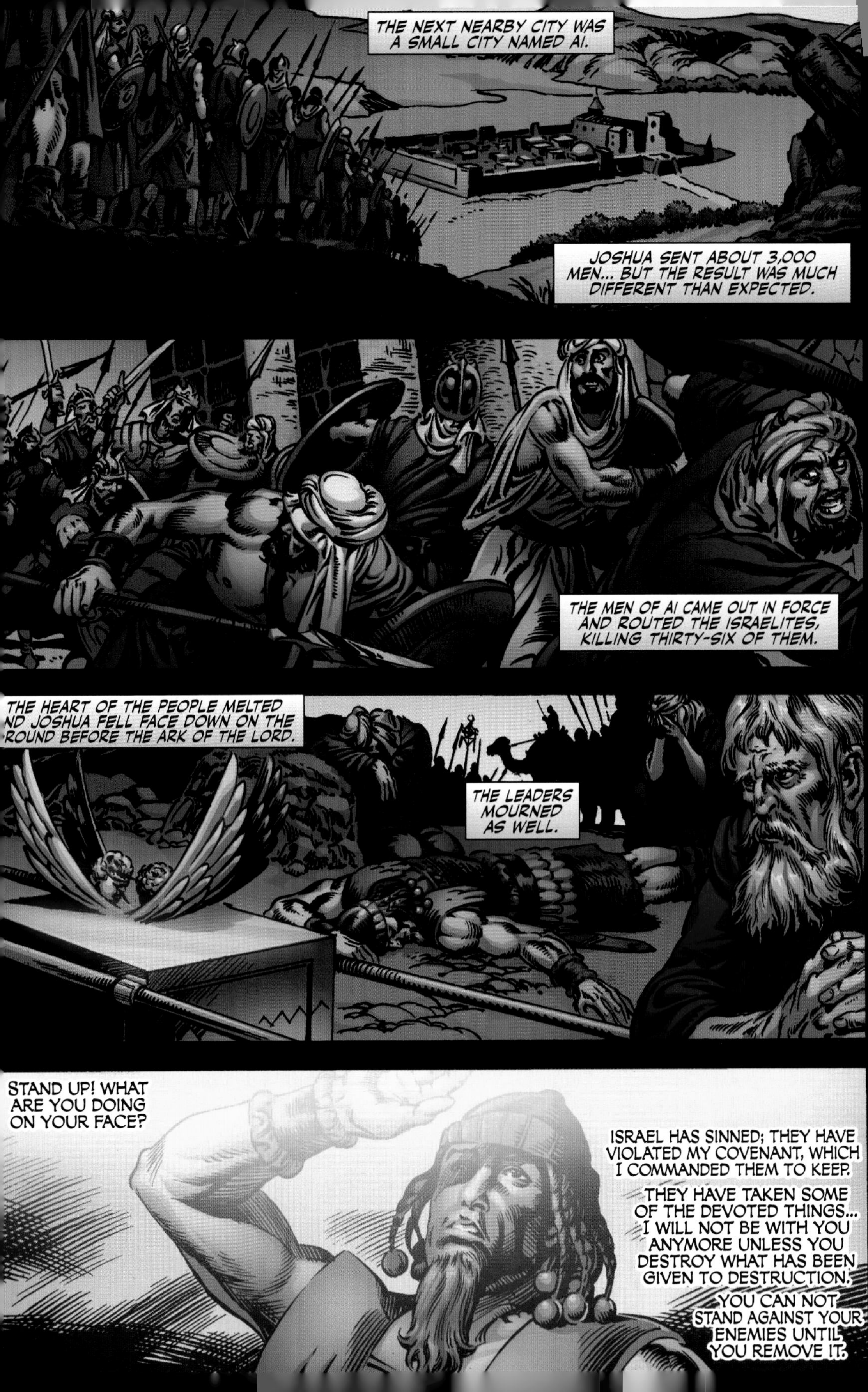
THE NEXT NEARBY CITY WAS A SMALL CITY NAMED AI.
JOSHUA SENT ABOUT 3,000 MEN... BUT THE RESULT WAS MUCH DIFFERENT THAN EXPECTED.
THE MEN OF AI CAME OUT IN FORCE AND ROUTED THE ISRAELITES, KILLING THIRTY-SIX OF THEM.
THE HEART OF THE PEOPLE MELTED ND JOSHUA FELL FACE DOWN ON THE ROUND BEFORE THE ARK OF THE LORD.
THE LEADERS MOURNED AS WELL.
STAND UP! WHAT ARE YOU DOING ON YOUR FACE?
ISRAEL HAS SINNED; THEY HAVE VIOLATED MY COVENANT, WHICH I COMMANDED THEM TO KEEP.
THEY HAVE TAKEN SOME OF THE DEVOTED THINGS... I WILL NOT BE WITH YOU ANYMORE UNLESS YOU DESTROY WHAT HAS BEEN GIVEN TO DESTRUCTION.
YOU CAN NOT STAND AGAINST YOUR ENEMIES UNTIL YOU REMOVE IT.

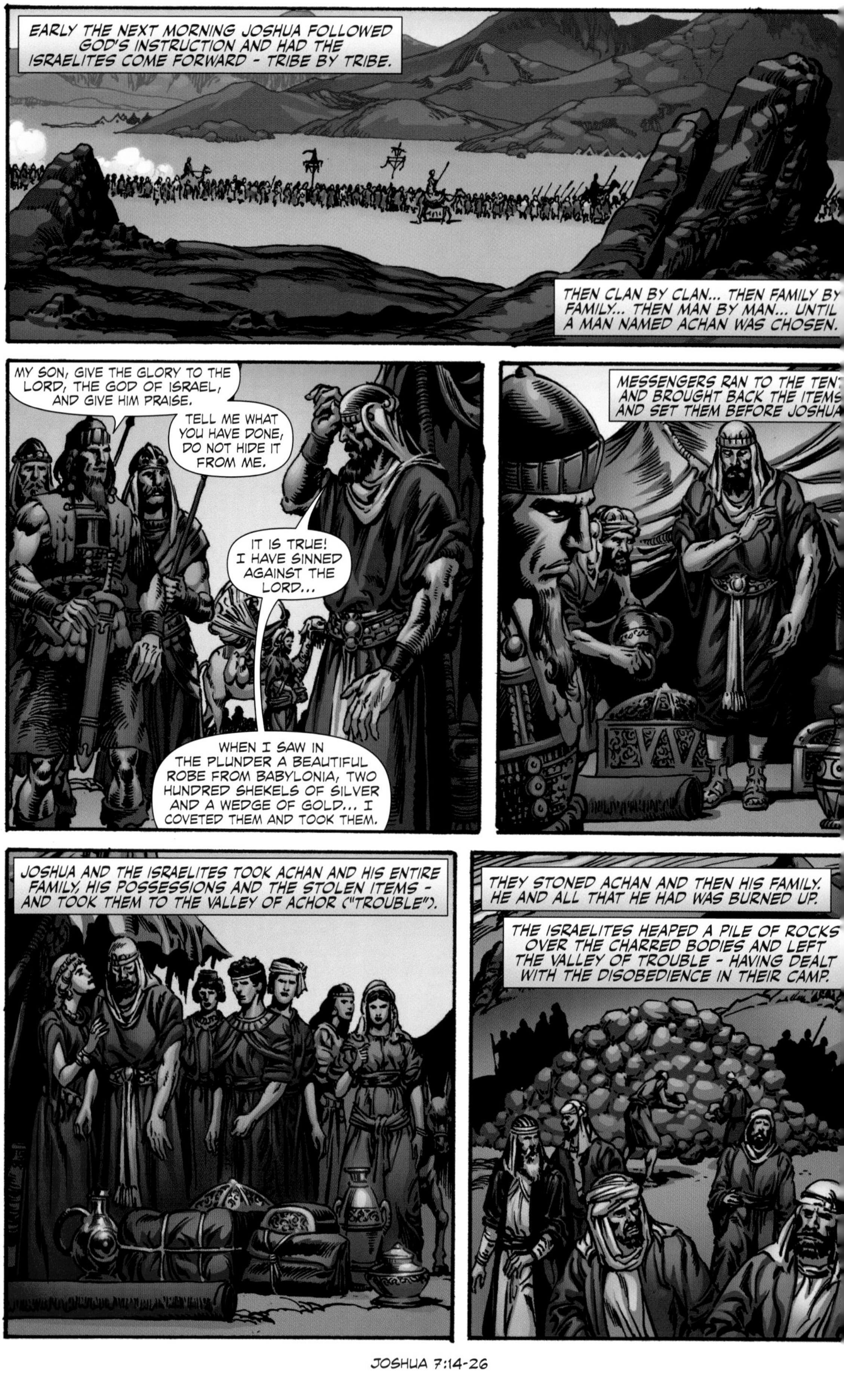
EARLY THE NEXT MORNING JOSHUA FOLLOWED GOD'S INSTRUCTION AND HAD THE ISRAELITES COME FORWARD - TRIBE BY TRIBE.
THEN CLAN BY CLAN... THEN FAMILY BY FAMILY... THEN MAN BY MAN... UNTIL A MAN NAMED ACHAN WAS CHOSEN.
MY SON, GIVE THE GLORY TO THE LORD, THE GOD OF ISRAEL, AND GIVE HIM PRAISE.
TELL ME WHAT YOU HAVE DONE, DO NOT HIDE IT FROM ME.
IT IS TRUE! I HAVE SINNED AGAINST THE LORD...
WHEN I SAW IN THE PLUNDER A BEAUTIFUL ROBE FROM BABYLONIA, TWO HUNDRED SHEKELS OF SILVER AND A WEDGE OF GOLD... I COVETED THEM AND TOOK THEM.
MESSENGERS RAN TO THE TENT AND BROUGHT BACK THE ITEMS AND SET THEM BEFORE JOSHUA
JOSHUA AND THE ISRAELITES TOOK ACHAN AND HIS ENTIRE FAMILY, HIS POSSESSIONS AND THE STOLEN ITEMS - AND TOOK THEM TO THE VALLEY OF ACHOR ("TROUBLE").
THEY STONED ACHAN AND THEN HIS FAMILY. HE AND ALL THAT HE HAD WAS BURNED UP.
THE ISRAELITES HEAPED A PILE OF ROCKS OVER THE CHARRED BODIES AND LEFT THE VALLEY OF TROUBLE - HAVING DEALT WITH THE DISOBEDIENCE IN THEIR CAMP.

JOSHUA 7:14-26

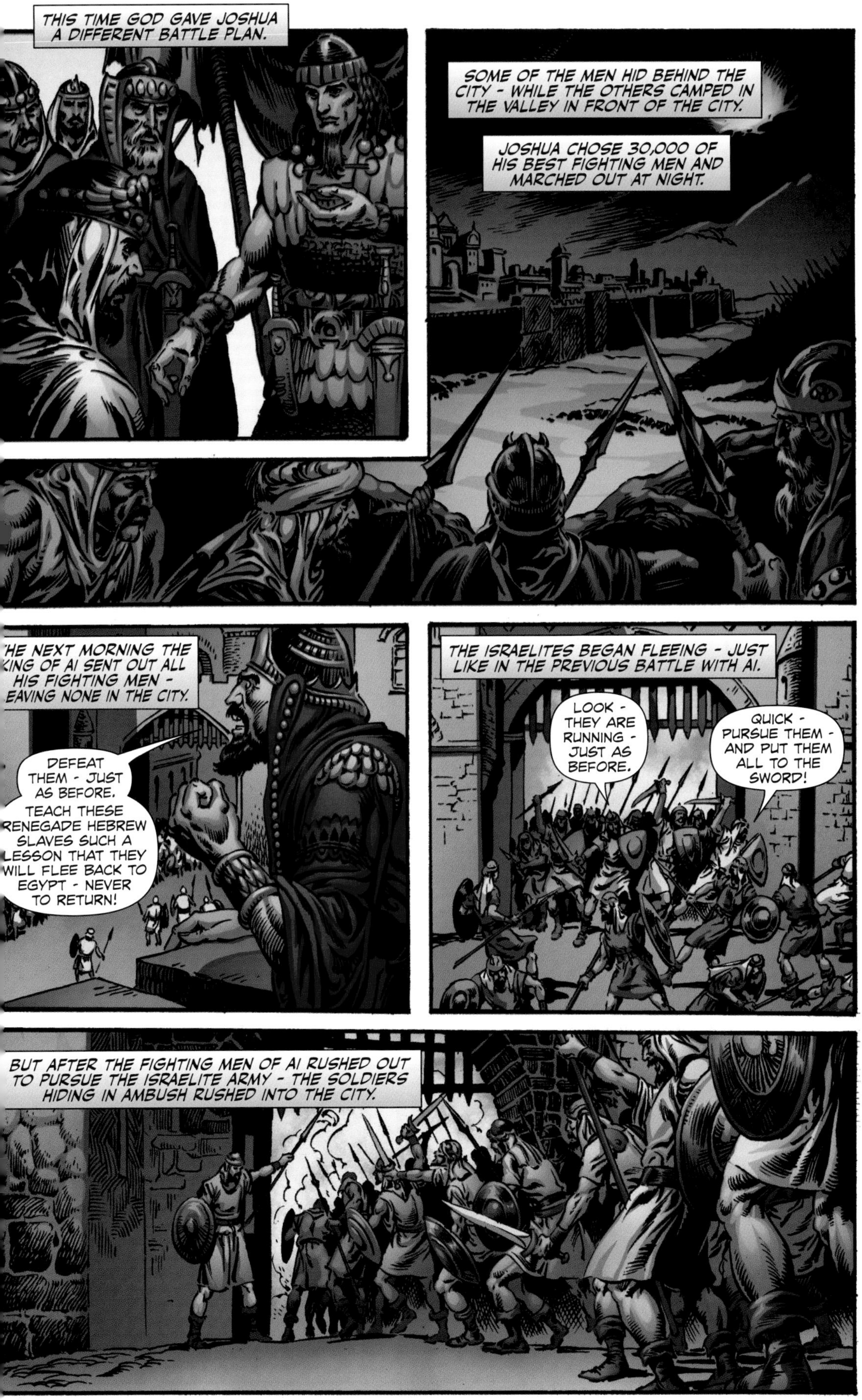
THIS TIME GOD GAVE JOSHUA A DIFFERENT BATTLE PLAN.
JOSHUA CHOSE 30,000 OF HIS BEST FIGHTING MEN AND MARCHED OUT AT NIGHT.
SOME OF THE MEN HID BEHIND THE CITY - WHILE THE OTHERS CAMPED IN THE VALLEY IN FRONT OF THE CITY.
HE NEXT MORNING THE KING OF AI SENT OUT ALL HIS FIGHTING MEN - EAVING NONE IN THE CITY.
DEFEAT THEM - JUST AS BEFORE. TEACH THESE RENEGADE HEBREW SLAVES SUCH A LESSON THAT THEY WILL FLEE BACK TO EGYPT - NEVER TO RETURN!
THE ISRAELITES BEGAN FLEEING - JUST LIKE IN THE PREVIOUS BATTLE WITH AI.
LOOK - THEY ARE RUNNING - JUST AS BEFORE.
QUICK - PURSUE THEM - AND PUT THEM ALL TO THE SWORD!
BUT AFTER THE FIGHTING MEN OF AI RUSHED OUT TO PURSUE THE ISRAELITE ARMY - THE SOLDIERS HIDING IN AMBUSH RUSHED INTO THE CITY.

JOSHUA 8:1-19

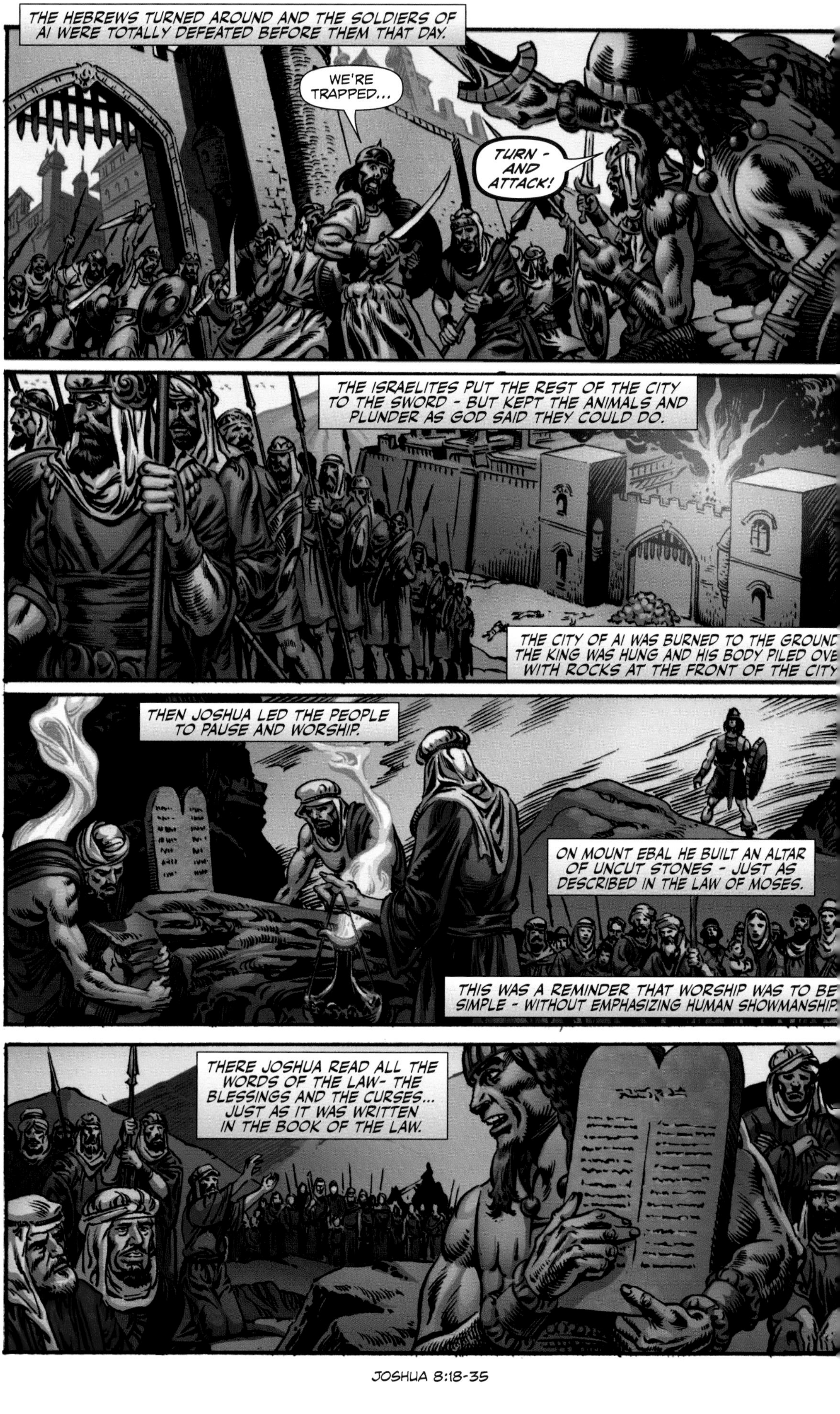
THE HEBREWS TURNED AROUND AND THE SOLDIERS OF AI WERE TOTALLY DEFEATED BEFORE THEM THAT DAY.
WE'RE TRAPPED...
TURN - AND ATTACK!
THE ISRAELITES PUT THE REST OF THE CITY TO THE SWORD - BUT KEPT THE ANIMALS AND PLUNDER AS GOD SAID THEY COULD DO.
THE CITY OF AI WAS BURNED TO THE GROUN
THE KING WAS HUNG AND HIS BODY PILED OVE
WITH ROCKS AT THE FRONT OF THE CITY
THEN JOSHUA LED THE PEOPLE TO PAUSE AND WORSHIP.
ON MOUNT EBAL HE BUILT AN ALTAR OF UNCUT STONES - JUST AS DESCRIBED IN THE LAW OF MOSES.
THIS WAS A REMINDER THAT WORSHIP WAS TO BE SIMPLE - WITHOUT EMPHASIZING HUMAN SHOWMANSHIP.
THERE JOSHUA READ ALL THE WORDS OF THE LAW- THE BLESSINGS AND THE CURSES... JUST AS IT WAS WRITTEN IN THE BOOK OF THE LAW.

JOSHUA 8:18-35

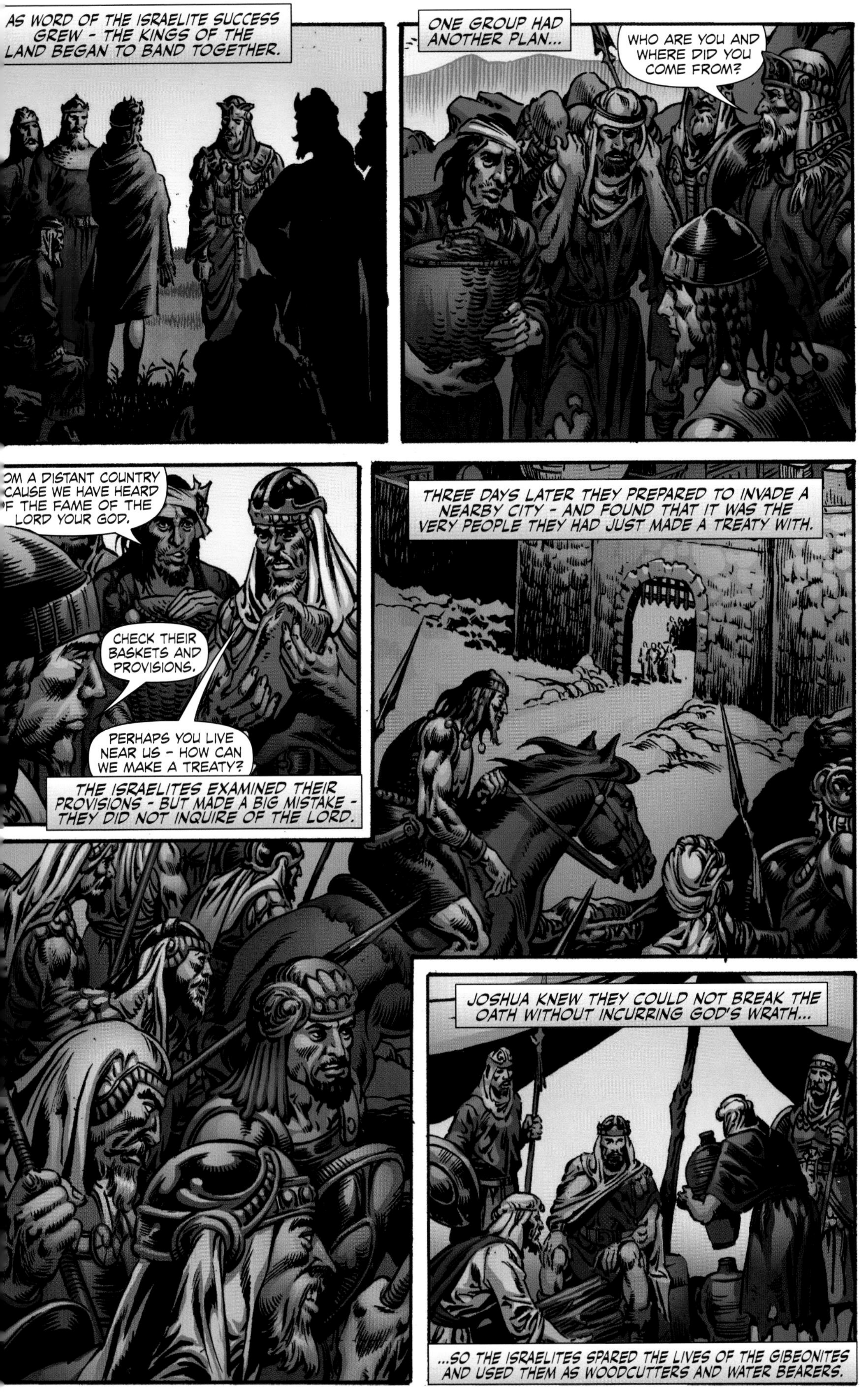
AS WORD OF THE ISRAELITE SUCCESS GREW - THE KINGS OF THE LAND BEGAN TO BAND TOGETHER.
ONE GROUP HAD ANOTHER PLAN...
WHO ARE YOU AND WHERE DID YOU COME FROM?
OM A DISTANT COUNTRY CAUSE WE HAVE HEARD F THE FAME OF THE LORD YOUR GOD.
CHECK THEIR BASKETS AND PROVISIONS.
PERHAPS YOU LIVE NEAR US - HOW CAN WE MAKE A TREATY?
THE ISRAELITES EXAMINED THEIR PROVISIONS - BUT MADE A BIG MISTAKE - THEY DID NOT INQUIRE OF THE LORD.
THREE DAYS LATER THEY PREPARED TO INVADE A NEARBY CITY - AND FOUND THAT IT WAS THE VERY PEOPLE THEY HAD JUST MADE A TREATY WITH.
JOSHUA KNEW THEY COULD NOT BREAK THE OATH WITHOUT INCURRING GOD'S WRATH...
...SO THE ISRAELITES SPARED THE LIVES OF THE GIBEONITES AND USED THEM AS WOODCUTTERS AND WATER BEARERS.

JOSHUA 9:1-27

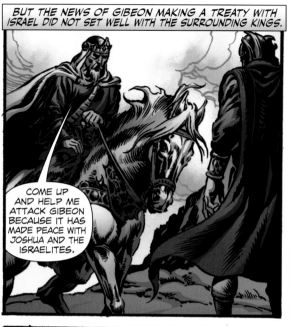

BUT THE NEWS OF GIBEON MAKING A TREATY WITH ISRAEL DID NOT SET WELL WITH THE SURROUNDING KINGS.

COME UP AND HELP ME ATTACK GIBEON BECAUSE IT HAS MADE PEACE WITH JOSHUA AND THE ISRAELITES.

SO THE FIVE MAIN KINGS OF THE AMORITES JOINED FORCES AND MOVED THEIR TROOPS TO SACK THE CITY OF GIBEON.

SEND WORD TO JOSHUA - HE MUST MOVE QUICKLY TO SAVE US.

ALL THE AMORITE KINGS HAVE JOINED FORCES AGAINST US.

QUICKLY, GATHER THE BEST FIGHTING MEN ALONG WITH ALL THE TROOPS.

GIBEON NEEDS HELP NOW.

DO NOT BE AFRAID OF THEM.

I HAVE GIVEN THEM INTO YOUR HAND.

NOT ONE OF THEM WILL BE ABLE TO WITHSTAND YOU.

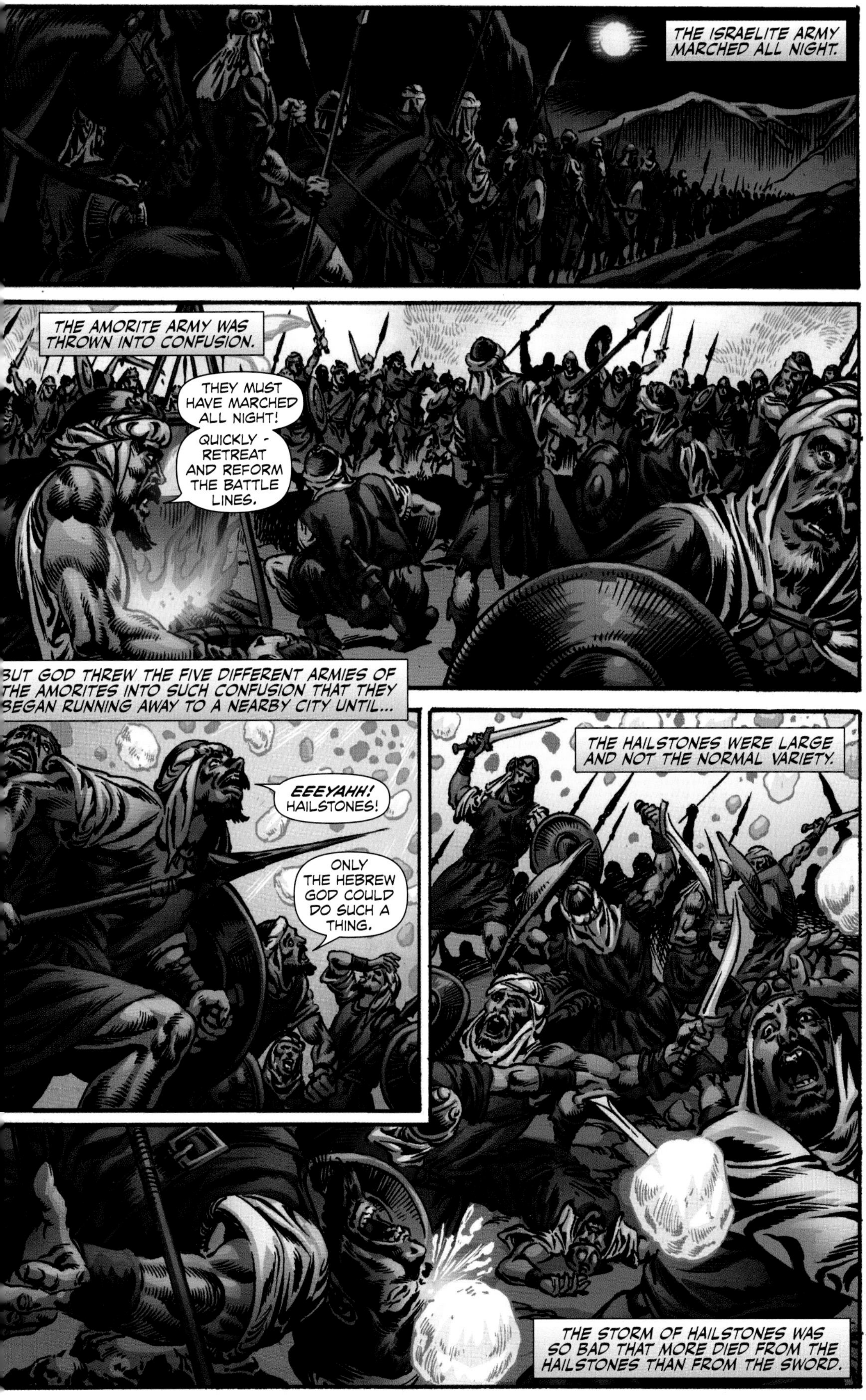
THE ISRAELITE ARMY MARCHED ALL NIGHT.
THE AMORITE ARMY WAS THROWN INTO CONFUSION.
THEY MUST HAVE MARCHED ALL NIGHT!
QUICKLY - RETREAT AND REFORM THE BATTLE LINES.
BUT GOD THREW THE FIVE DIFFERENT ARMIES OF THE AMORITES INTO SUCH CONFUSION THAT THEY BEGAN RUNNING AWAY TO A NEARBY CITY UNTIL...
EEEYAHH! HAILSTONES!
ONLY THE HEBREW GOD COULD DO SUCH A THING.
THE HAILSTONES WERE LARGE AND NOT THE NORMAL VARIETY.
THE STORM OF HAILSTONES WAS SO BAD THAT MORE DIED FROM THE HAILSTONES THAN FROM THE SWORD.

JOSHUA 10:9-11

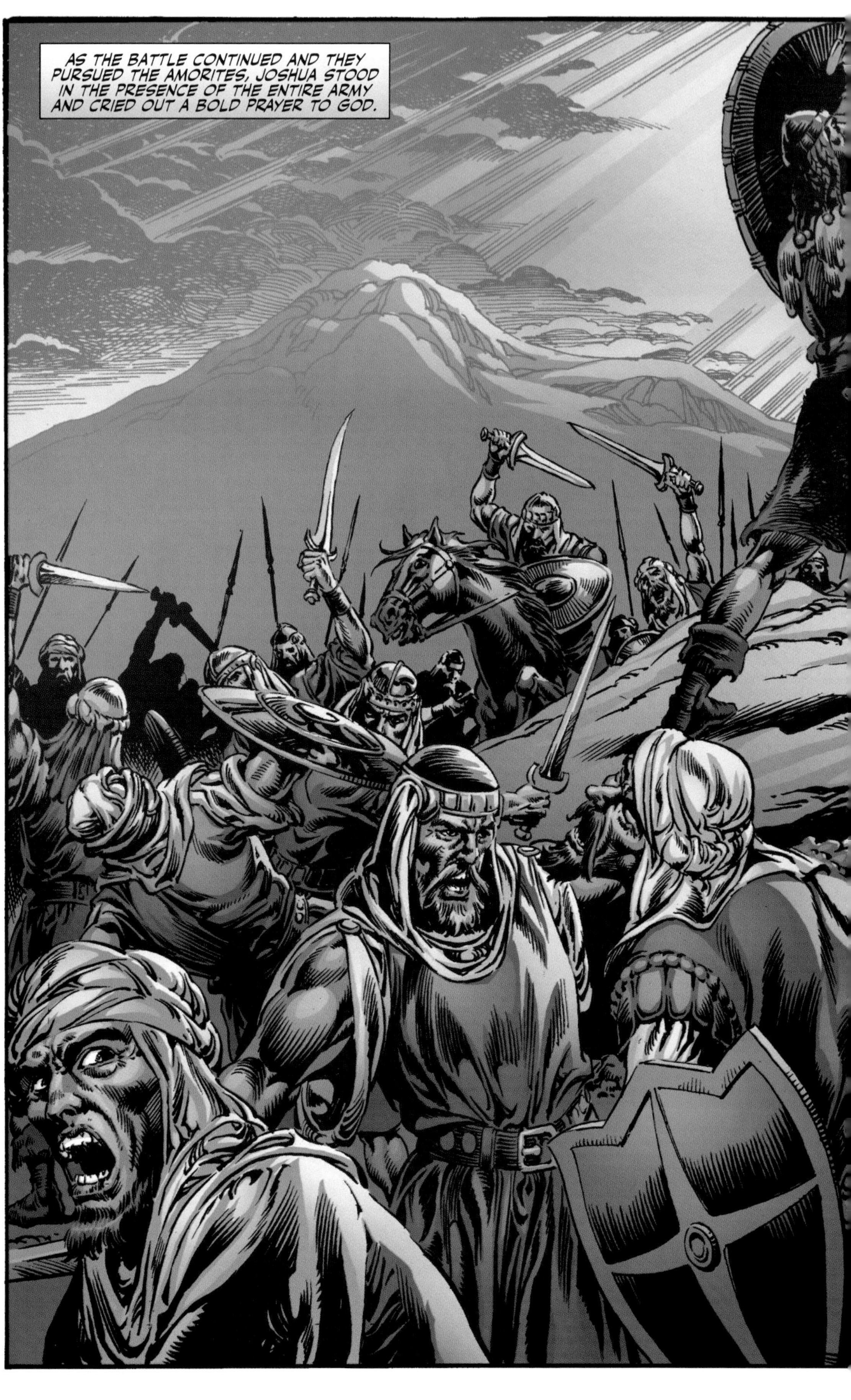
AS THE BATTLE CONTINUED AND THEY PURSUED THE AMORITES, JOSHUA STOOD IN THE PRESENCE OF THE ENTIRE ARMY AND CRIED OUT A BOLD PRAYER TO GOD.

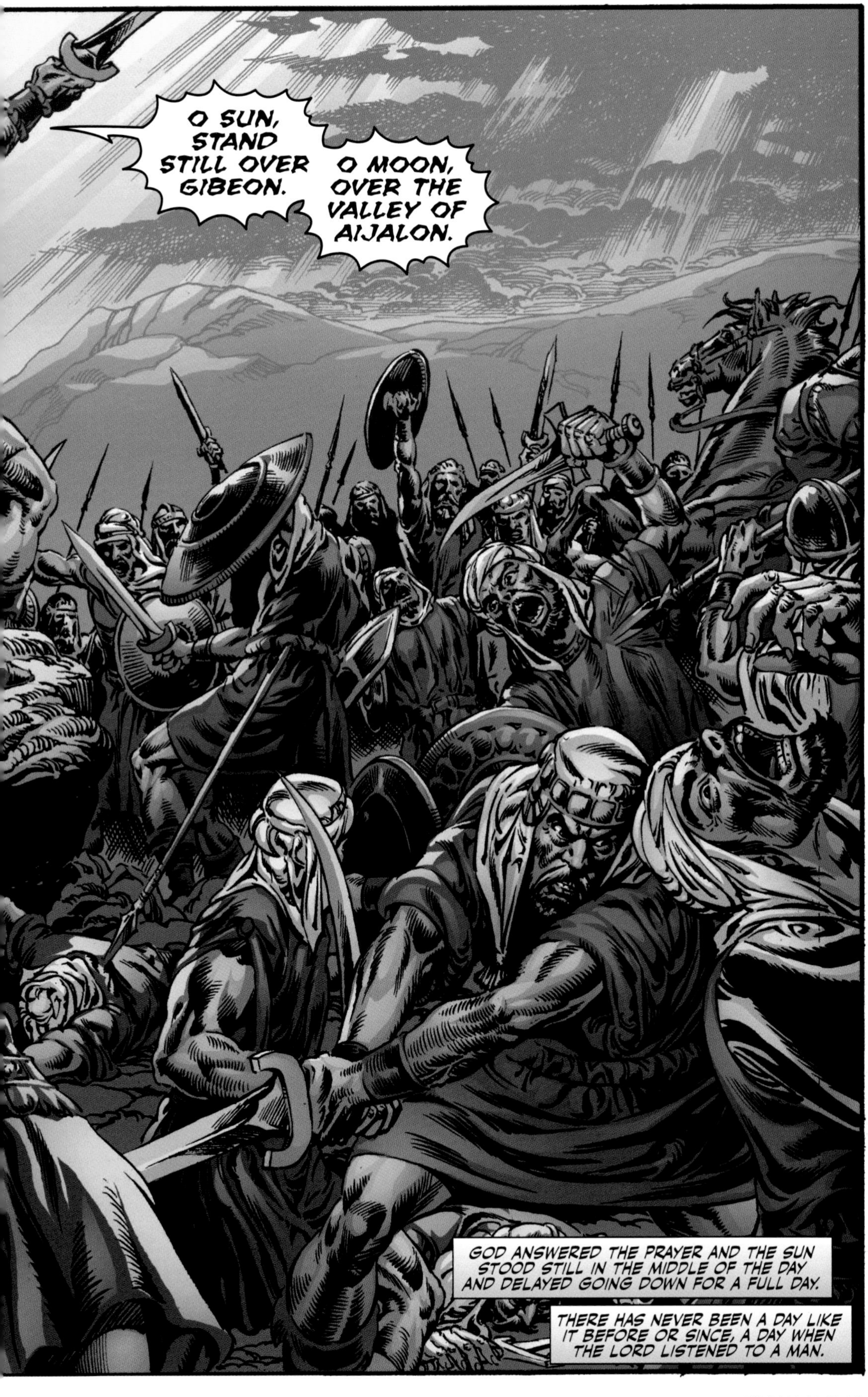
O SUN, STAND STILL OVER GIBEON.
O MOON, OVER THE VALLEY OF AIJALON.
GOD ANSWERED THE PRAYER AND THE SUN STOOD STILL IN THE MIDDLE OF THE DAY AND DELAYED GOING DOWN FOR A FULL DAY.
THERE HAS NEVER BEEN A DAY LIKE IT BEFORE OR SINCE, A DAY WHEN THE LORD LISTENED TO A MAN.

JOSHUA 10:12-14

AFTER THE COMPLETE VICTORY, JOSHUA AND ALL THE SOLDIERS RETURNED TO THEIR CAMP AT GILGAL.

THE FIVE AMORITE KINGS HAVE HIDDEN THEM-SELVES IN THE CAVE AT MAKKEDAH.

ROLL LARGE ROCKS UP TO THE MOUTH OF THE CAVE AND POST MEN TO GUARD IT.

...BUT KEEP PURSUING THE ENEMY BEFORE THEY REACH THEIR FORTIFIED CITIES.

BRING OUT THE KINGS TO ME.

DO NOT BE AFRAID. DO NOT BE DIS-COURAGED.

BE STRONG AND COURAGEOUS. THIS IS WHAT THE LORD WILL DO TO ALL THE ENEMIES YOU WILL FIGHT.

AND THE WORD OF THE LORD THROUGH JOSHUA PROVED TRUE.

OVER THE NEXT SEVERAL YEARS JOSHUA AND THE HEBREW ARMIES CONQUERED THE SOUTHERN CITIES IN THE LAND OF CANAAN.

THEY ALSO CONQUERED THE NORTHERN KINGS AND THEIR CITIES.

JOSHUA 10:15-12:24

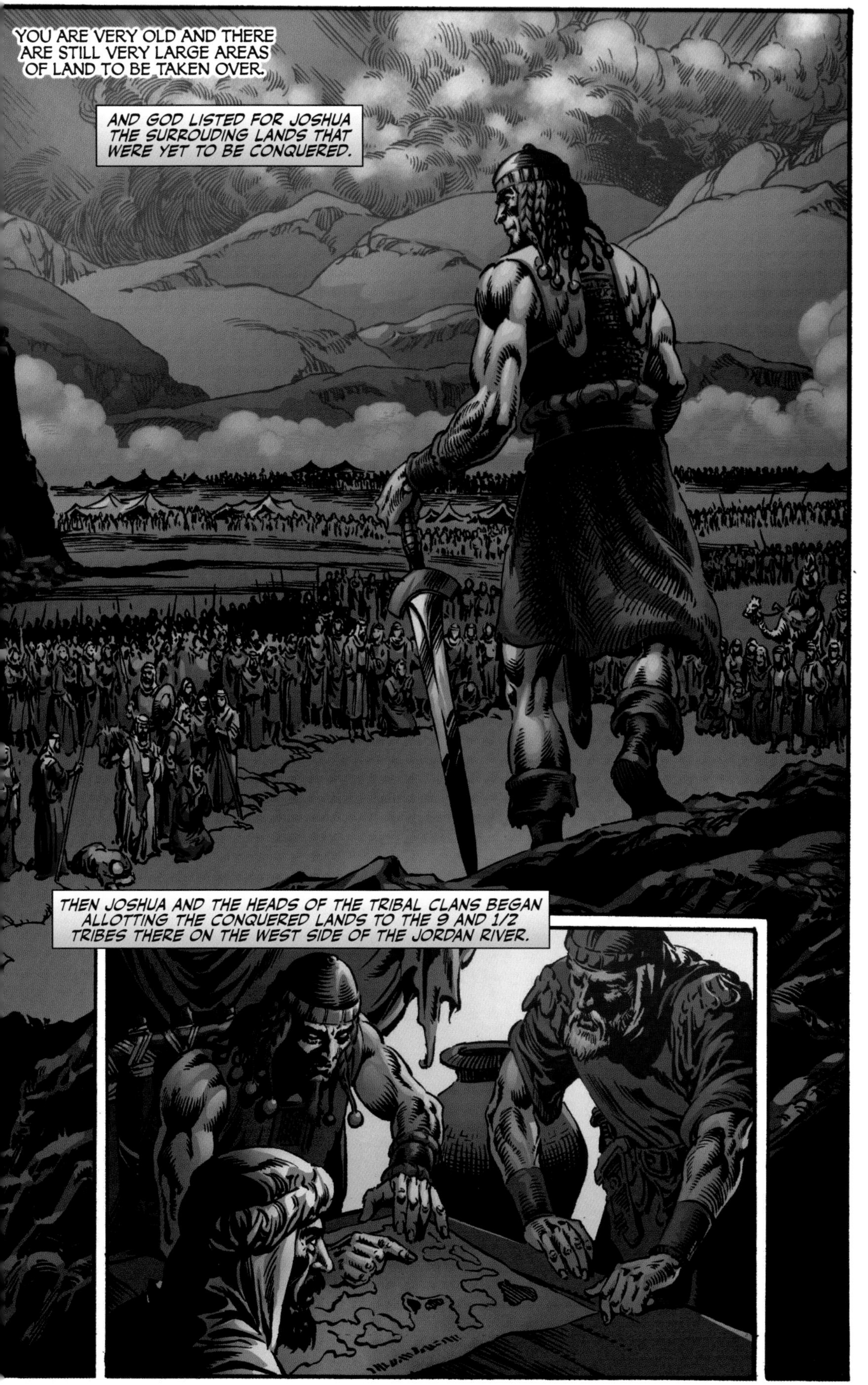
YOU ARE VERY OLD AND THERE ARE STILL VERY LARGE AREAS OF LAND TO BE TAKEN OVER.
AND GOD LISTED FOR JOSHUA THE SURROUDING LANDS THAT WERE YET TO BE CONQUERED.
THEN JOSHUA AND THE HEADS OF THE TRIBAL CLANS BEGAN ALLOTTING THE CONQUERED LANDS TO THE 9 AND 1/2 TRIBES THERE ON THE WEST SIDE OF THE JORDAN RIVER.

JOSHUA 13:1-7

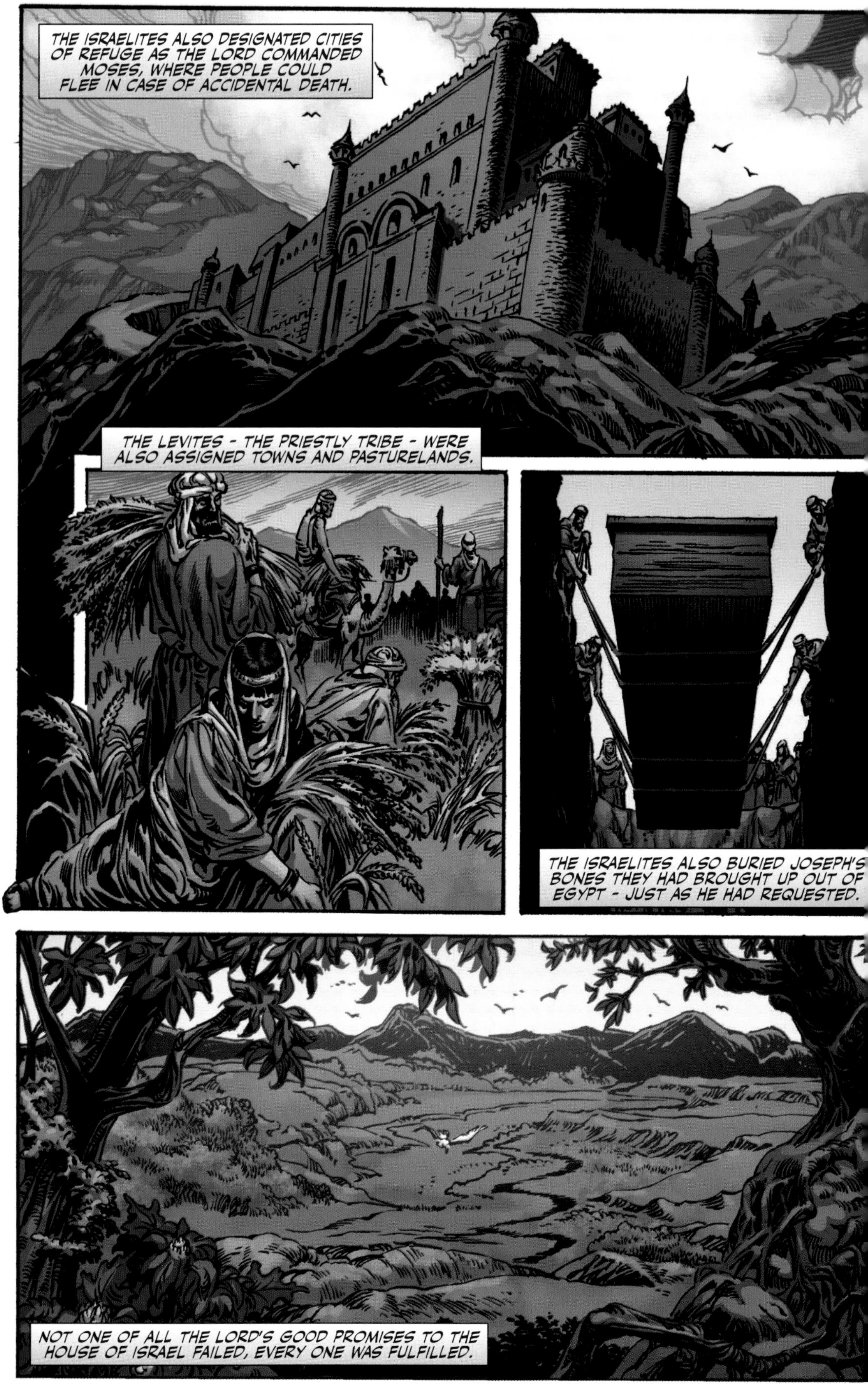
THE ISRAELITES ALSO DESIGNATED CITIES OF REFUGE AS THE LORD COMMANDED MOSES, WHERE PEOPLE COULD FLEE IN CASE OF ACCIDENTAL DEATH.
THE LEVITES - THE PRIESTLY TRIBE - WERE ALSO ASSIGNED TOWNS AND PASTURELANDS.
THE ISRAELITES ALSO BURIED JOSEPH'S BONES THEY HAD BROUGHT UP OUT OF EGYPT - JUST AS HE HAD REQUESTED.
NOT ONE OF ALL THE LORD'S GOOD PROMISES TO THE HOUSE OF ISRAEL FAILED, EVERY ONE WAS FULFILLED.

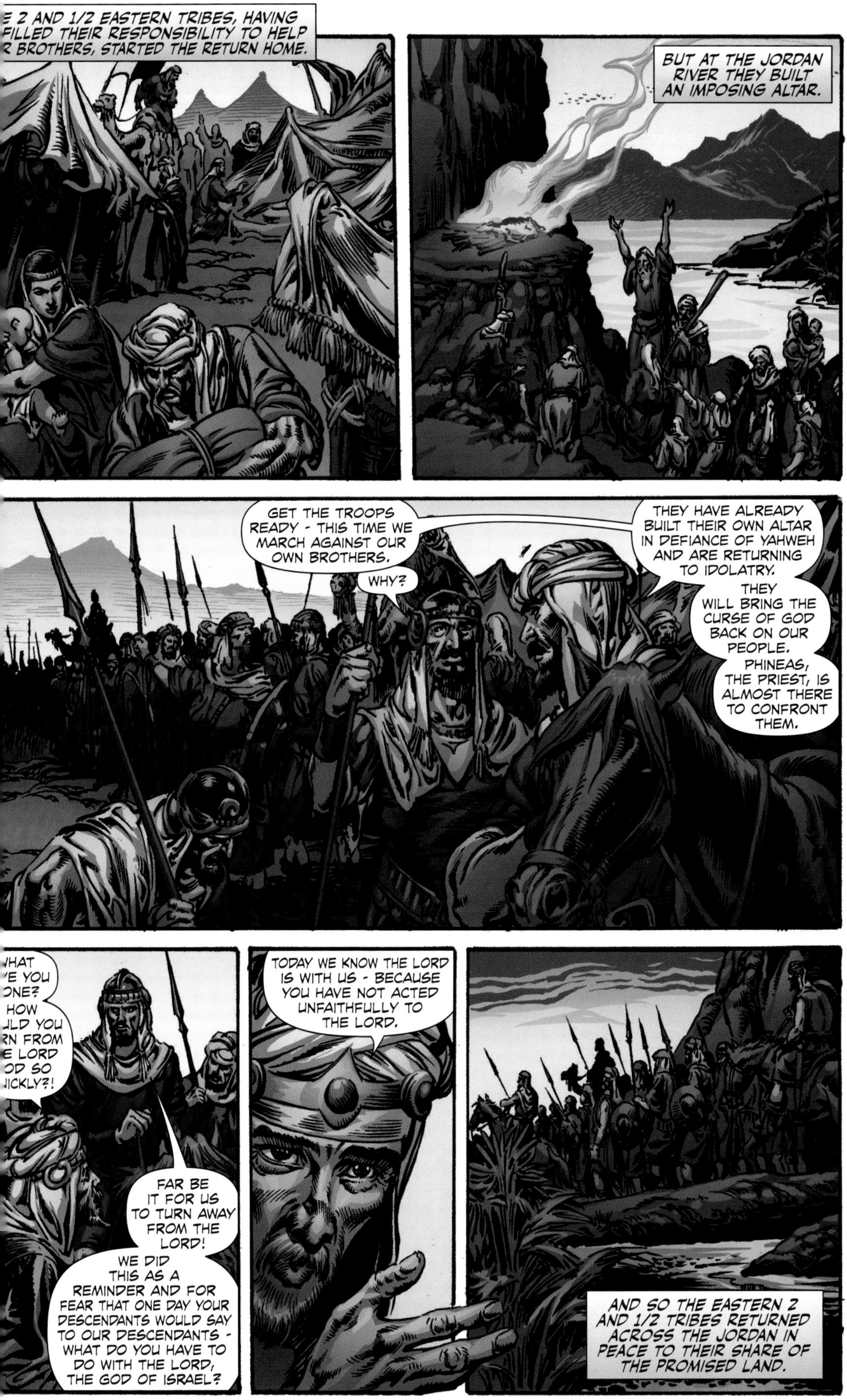
E 2 AND 1/2 EASTERN TRIBES, HAVING FILLED THEIR RESPONSIBILITY TO HELP R BROTHERS, STARTED THE RETURN HOME.
BUT AT THE JORDAN RIVER THEY BUILT AN IMPOSING ALTAR.
GET THE TROOPS READY - THIS TIME WE MARCH AGAINST OUR OWN BROTHERS.
WHY?
THEY HAVE ALREADY BUILT THEIR OWN ALTAR IN DEFIANCE OF YAHWEH AND ARE RETURNING TO IDOLATRY.
THEY WILL BRING THE CURSE OF GOD BACK ON OUR PEOPLE.
PHINEAS, THE PRIEST, IS ALMOST THERE TO CONFRONT THEM.
HAT E YOU ONE? HOW LD YOU RN FROM E LORD OD SO ICKLY?!
FAR BE IT FOR US TO TURN AWAY FROM THE LORD!
WE DID THIS AS A REMINDER AND FOR FEAR THAT ONE DAY YOUR DESCENDANTS WOULD SAY TO OUR DESCENDANTS - WHAT DO YOU HAVE TO DO WITH THE LORD, THE GOD OF ISRAEL?
TODAY WE KNOW THE LORD IS WITH US - BECAUSE YOU HAVE NOT ACTED UNFAITHFULLY TO THE LORD.
AND SO THE EASTERN 2 AND 1/2 TRIBES RETURNED ACROSS THE JORDAN IN PEACE TO THEIR SHARE OF THE PROMISED LAND.

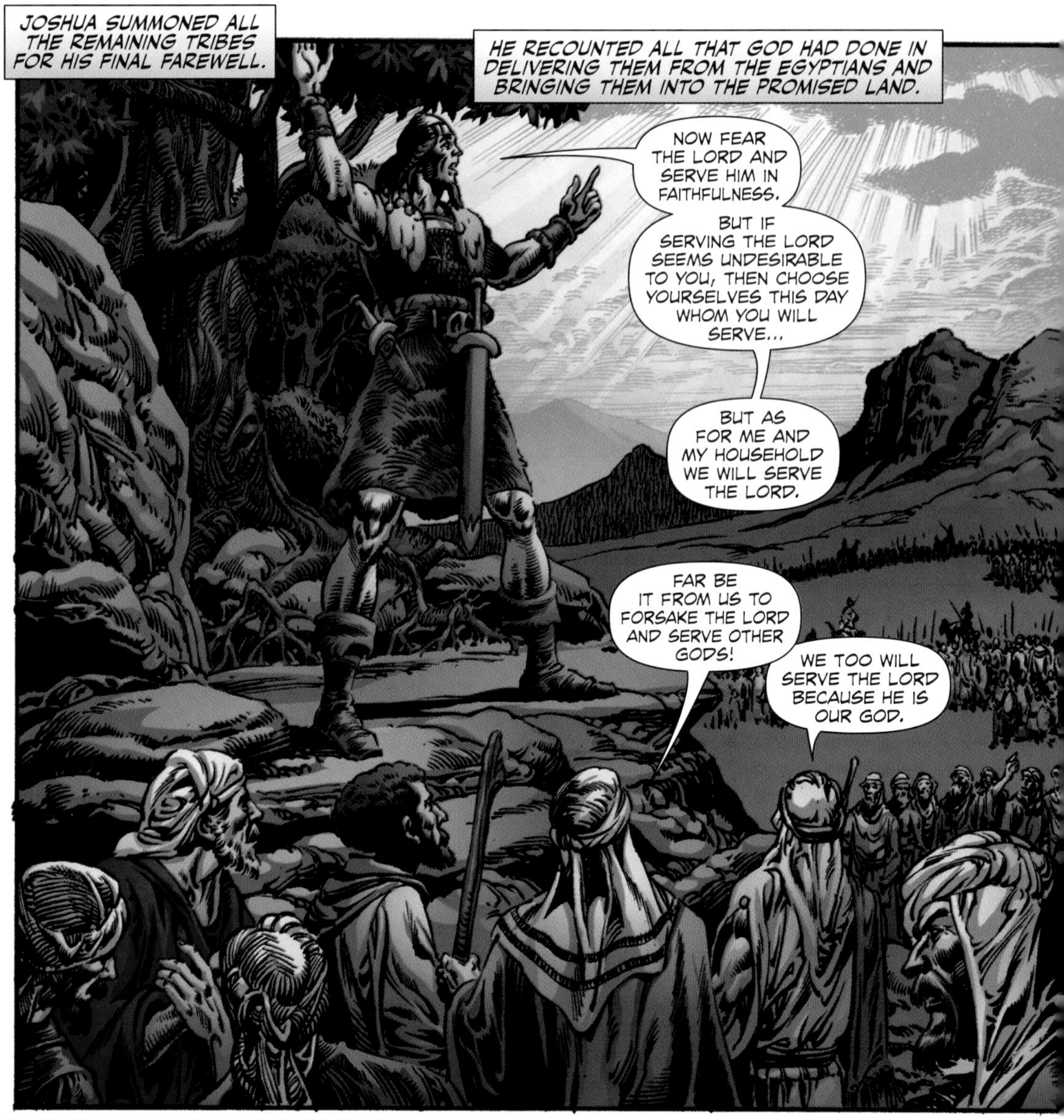
JOSHUA SUMMONED ALL THE REMAINING TRIBES FOR HIS FINAL FAREWELL.
HE RECOUNTED ALL THAT GOD HAD DONE IN DELIVERING THEM FROM THE EGYPTIANS AND BRINGING THEM INTO THE PROMISED LAND.
NOW FEAR THE LORD AND SERVE HIM IN FAITHFULNESS.
BUT IF SERVING THE LORD SEEMS UNDESIRABLE TO YOU, THEN CHOOSE YOURSELVES THIS DAY WHOM YOU WILL SERVE...
BUT AS FOR ME AND MY HOUSEHOLD WE WILL SERVE THE LORD.
FAR BE IT FROM US TO FORSAKE THE LORD AND SERVE OTHER GODS!
WE TOO WILL SERVE THE LORD BECAUSE HE IS OUR GOD.

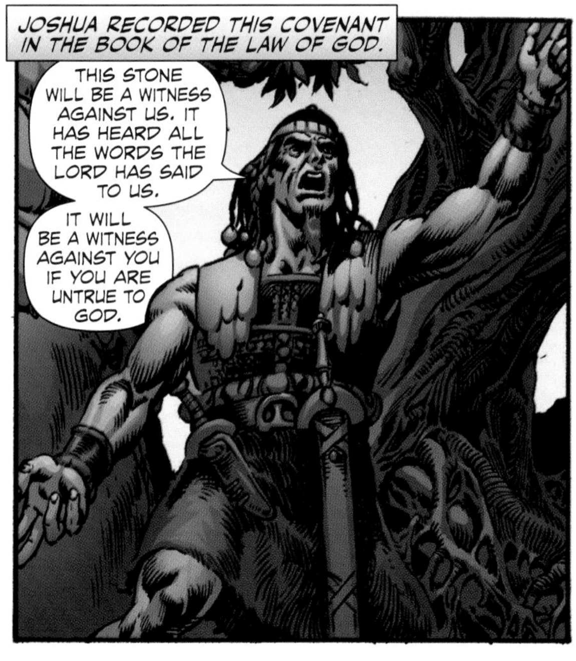
JOSHUA RECORDED THIS COVENANT IN THE BOOK OF THE LAW OF GOD.
THIS STONE WILL BE A WITNESS AGAINST US. IT HAS HEARD ALL THE WORDS THE LORD HAS SAID TO US.
IT WILL BE A WITNESS AGAINST YOU IF YOU ARE UNTRUE TO GOD.

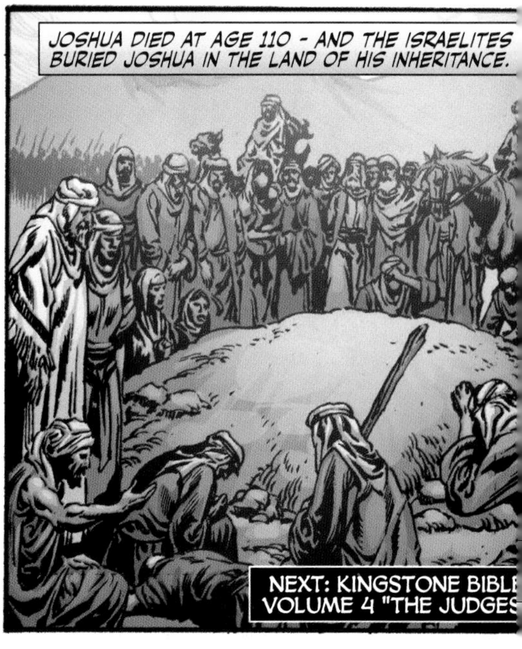
JOSHUA DIED AT AGE 110 - AND THE ISRAELITES BURIED JOSHUA IN THE LAND OF HIS INHERITANCE.
NEXT: KINGSTONE BIBL
VOLUME 4 "THE JUDGES

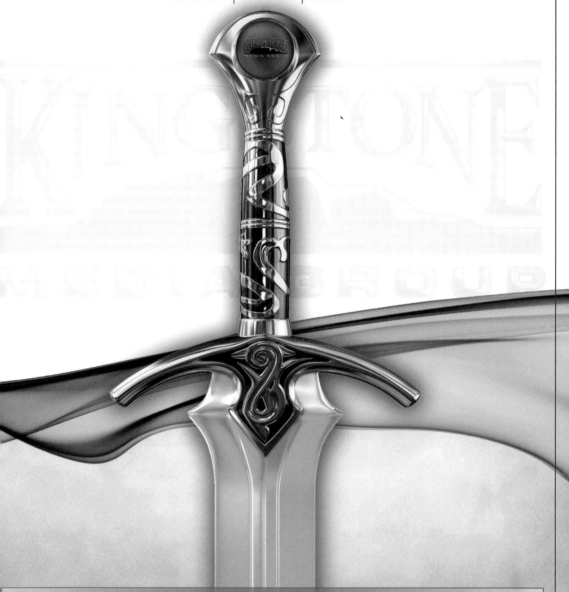

KINGSTONE COMICS

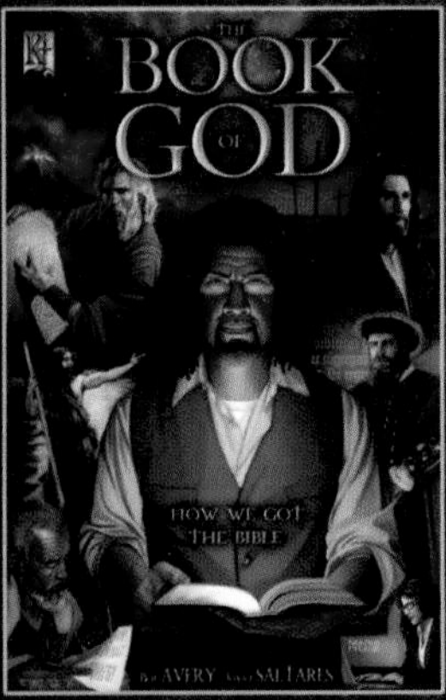
THE BOOK OF GOD
HOW WE GOT THE BIBLE

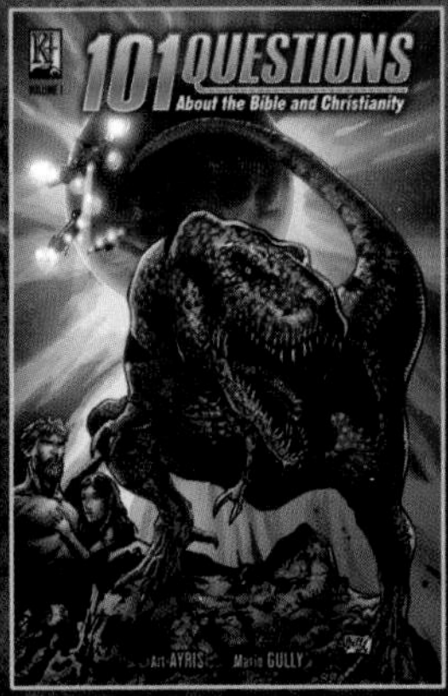
101 QUESTIONS
About the Bible and Christianity
Art AYRIS Mario GULLY

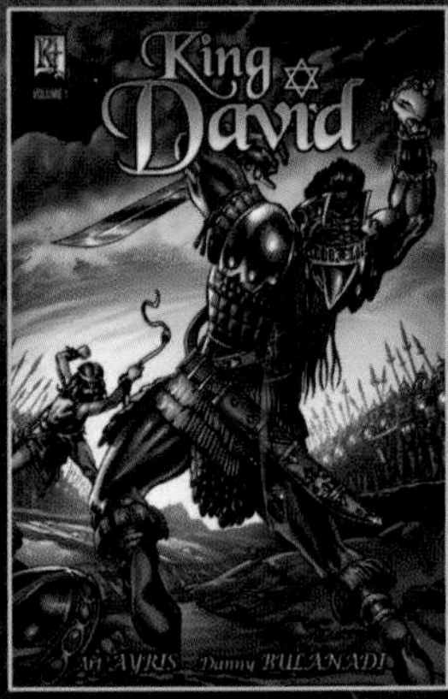
King David
Art AYRIS Danny BULANADI

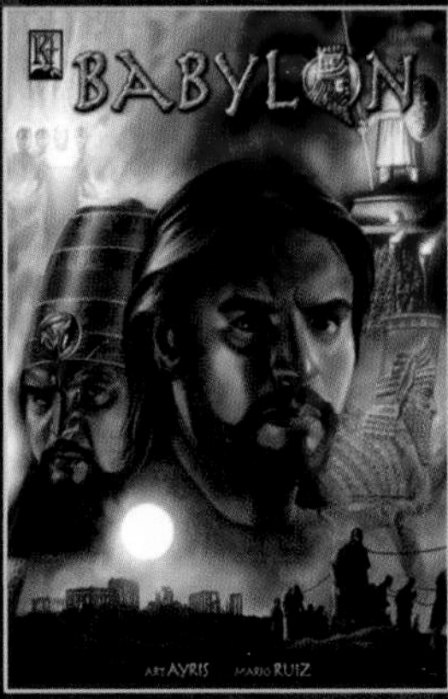
BABYLON
ART AYRIS MARIO RUIZ

THE HIGHEST VALUES IN ***CHRISTIAN COMICS***

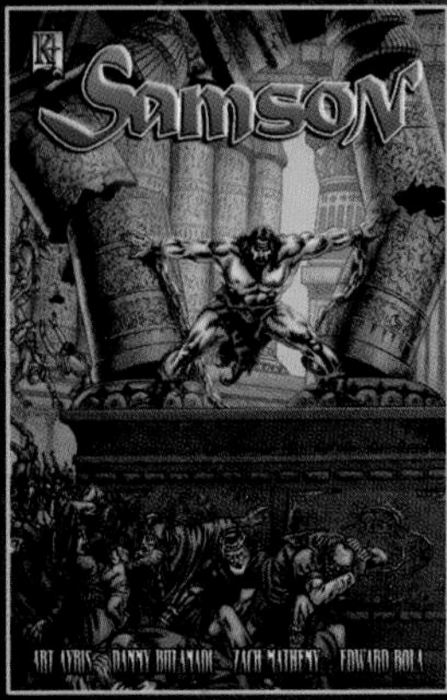
Samson
ART AYRIS DANNY BULANADI ZACH MATHENY EDWARD BOLA

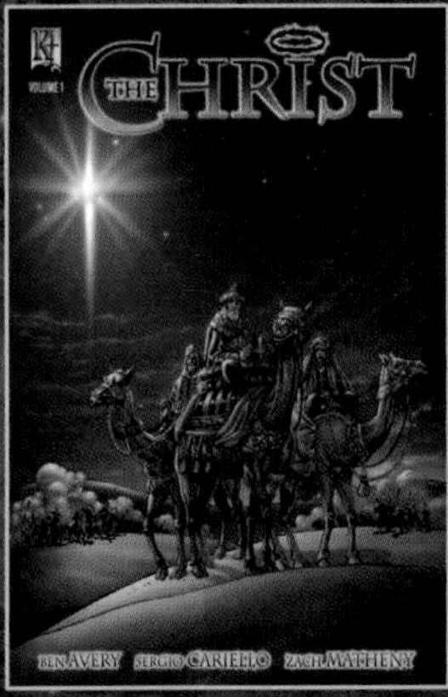
THE CHRIST
BEN AVERY SERGIO CARIELLO ZACH MATHENY

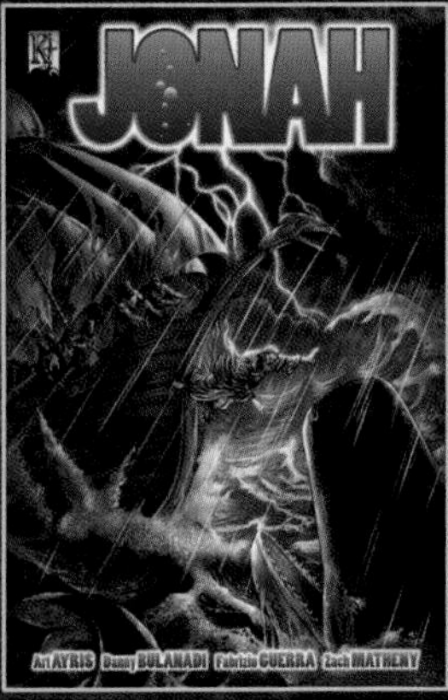
JONAH
Art AYRIS Danny BULANADI Fabricio GUERRA Zach MATHENY

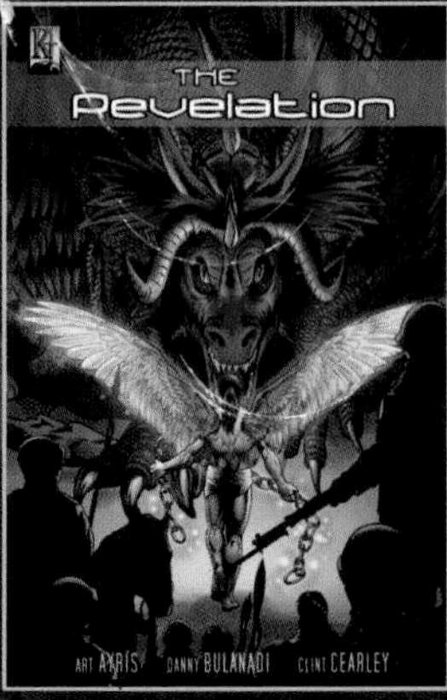
THE Revelation
ART AYRIS DANNY BULANADI CLINT CEARLEY

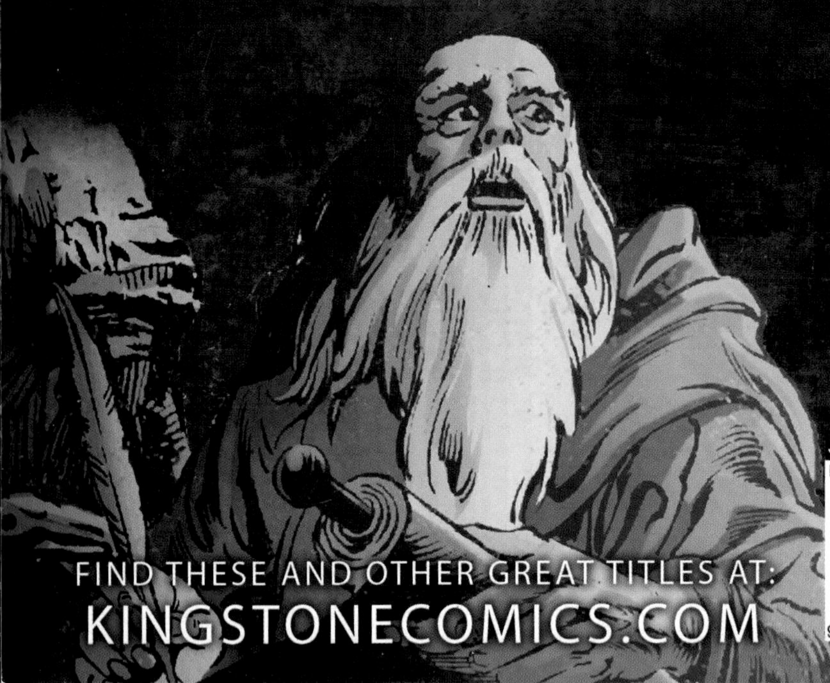

FIND THESE AND OTHER GREAT TITLES AT:
KINGSTONECOMICS.COM

Joshua
ISBN 978-1-61328-099-7 USD $3.99